SECOND CHANCE

To Jean,

Who does most of the work while
I do most of the talking.

SECOND CHANCE

*The Affectionate Story of One Family's
Efforts to Heal Sick Birds and Marine
Mammals and Return Them to the Wild*

ALAN BRYANT

*Drawings by
Steven Jaremko*

ST. MARTIN'S PRESS
NEW YORK

Library of Congress Cataloging in Publication Data

Bryant, Alan.
  Second chance.

    1. Wildlife rescue—Wales.   I. Title.
QL83.2.B78   1982   639.9   82-17074
ISBN 0-312-70828-9

First published in Great Britain by J.M. Dent & Sons Ltd.

First U.S. Edition
10 9 8 7 6 5 4 3 2 1

Preface

This book is the story of one family's efforts to treat sick birds
and marine mammals. My wife, Jean, and I, operate a little unit
called the New Quay Bird Hospital, on the west Wales coast,
dedicated primarily to the treatment of oiled seabirds but in
practice treating all kinds of birds. As a second and equally
natural progression, it now deals with Atlantic grey seals as
well, and on two never-to-be-forgotten occasions, dolphins.
There are few activities of the unit which don't involve the two
of us, as the frequent use of the pronoun 'we' in the narrative
shows.

Neither of us has any professional qualifications in the
treatment of anything, and we get nothing out of it but a good
deal of pleasure and satisfaction when things go right. To cover
the deficiency in our learning, we rely very heavily on the
veterinary profession, most particularly on our regular vet,
Tom Herbert of Aberaeron. Without him we would never have
started, and without his constant support, day or night, rain or
shine, we couldn't have carried on. Sometimes, when we get
involved in a rescue away from home, we have asked other vets
for help. Never once have we met reluctance to help, let alone
refusal, and never once have we have been charged by a vet for
help over a wild creature. We proclaim our thanks and appreciation to the world of vets in general and to Tom Herbert in
particular.

Treating wild birds gives us a unique opportunity of seeing them at close quarters. We have thrilled to the patterns of the barn owl's plumage, the amazing legs and feet of the grebe, the friendliness of the puffin and the austere dignity of the gannet. We watch, enthralled, the grace and dexterity of a baby seal. We get a tremendous kick, of course, when we realease to its proper environment a patient we have treated, confident that it is perfectly fit to go. Fortunately, this happens quite often.

In wildlife treatment units, as in most things, small is beautiful. The operation is viable only as long as one family can run it routinely. When it grows beyond that point there arises the dread spectre of the need for salaried help and consequent escalation in expenditure, something its fund-raising ability may not be able to meet. The answer, of course, is more small units, and we are exceedingly lucky in that some friends, Jean and Guy Haines, have recently set up a unit like ours near the town of Pembroke. There is plenty of room for outfits like our own. Outside oiling incidents, where transport is organized and distance is not such a problem, we get few birds from more than twenty miles away, which suggests that there is a need for such units dotted all over the country at about forty-mile intervals.

We can deal, as a family, with our routine intake of patients, but in emergencies, as when many birds are affected in an oiling incident, friends, neighbours and often complete strangers come to help. They help handle the birds, to collect them, and even do the housework to free Jean for more important things. We rely very largely on local contributions to finance the operation, raised mainly by an annual Open Day, and we are wonderfully supported by people who bring us things to sell, who come here to sell them and who come to buy. The clear leader in the first group is Jean's aunt in America, who sends so much stuff to sell that we now always have an 'Aunt Stella stall' at the open day. By no means the least of the joys of operating a wildlife treatment unit is the evidence it brings that there are many kind-hearted people in the world. This is the perfect place to thank them all, very sincerely, for the help they have given us over the years.

Contents

List of Plates

Photographs by Richard Waite and Alan Bryant

SECOND CHANCE

1

Moses the Seal

'Is that the Bird Hospital?' said the voice on the telephone, very faintly. 'Yes,' I answered, 'Alan Bryant speaking.'

'A baby seal has been lying on the beach at Aberporth for three days, next to a big dead one. Poor little thing, it wasn't getting a minute's peace, dogs were after it all the time.'

The speaker paused.

'Yes?' I said, encouragingly.

'Well, we've brought it home to try to look after it. We couldn't just leave it there. We wondered——'

'Yes?'

'Well, we were wondering if you had any fish handy to feed it.'

We had plenty, I replied. I identified the caller as a Mrs Peggram, wrote down her address, grabbed some fresh sprats and a stone of frozen ones and shot out of the front door into the car. Usually in emergencies Jean comes with me, but she was making jam at the time and the current batch was likely to go critical at any moment. So, for once, I went on my own. I was beating on Mrs Peggrams's door inside twenty minutes, and she led me to the baby seal.

Jean and I often watch seals in the wild. From the cliff-tops of the Pembrokeshire coast you can see them playing at quite considerable depths in the beautifully clear water below, and the grace of their movements would inspire a ballet company. Watching them in their own environment has put us off zoos for life. The youngsters are as lively as kittens in the sea, while ashore, they lie on their backs, flippers crossed on their chests, the very picture of confidence and contentment. Seals are superbly streamlined, of course, but they are also amazingly fat. Under the skin they have a layer of blubber which serves as a food reserve – a 'beachmaster' bull eats nothing for a couple of months in the breeding season – and provides body insulation from the cold water as well.

Baby seals are fatter than adults. We had only once been really close to a baby seal, which we were told had been in-jured, and we had gone off like crusaders to rescue it. It turned out perfectly fit, with a red stain on it, obviously applied by a researcher to ensure he only counted it once, which our infor-mant had mistakingly thought was blood. It was a bit over three feet long, about eighteen inches thick in the middle, and its front flippers hardly showed outside its body. With its huge round eyes and cheerful expression it looked very endearing and I picked it up without hesitation, my hands around its middle. It made a good deal of noise while I turned it over to examine it, and it made great play with a magnificent set of teeth, but being so very fat it couldn't turn its head far enough to get at my hands. I thought it was being playful, like a puppy.

This was my only experience of a seal until I got to Mrs Peggram, so the appearance of the baby in her back kitchen came as a tremendous shock. It had a hunted look, its head was too big for its thin, little body, its skin was badly cut in many places and it was having trouble breathing. Its eyes, which should have looked like saucers, were merely slits, and its breath was unbelievably foul. I was still under the happy delusion that baby seals were cuddly, gentle creatures, so I offered this one a sprat, in my fingers. He swung his head round with the speed of a striking snake and I fairly leapt back. It was as if a friendly but hungry pussy had suddenly turned into a Bengal tiger. There was nothing cuddly about this seal.

As I learned later, baby grey seals are not generally cuddly. Most of them will regard any approach by a human being as a threat and will respond thoroughly aggressively, even dangerously. The only safe way to pick one up is by the tail. Usually, the absence of aggression in a baby seal indicates extreme weakness, not a friendly spirit.

Now Jean and I had already had quite a lot of experience of treating birds, particulary oiled sea birds, but our knowledge hitherto of treating sick seals was theoretical, being confined to reading *Orphans of the Sea* by Ken Jones, who devotes his life to looking after seals in Cornwall. People in our area, like Mrs Peggram I guess, knew of our work with birds, and simply assumed we knew all about other animals too, even though this was far from being so. Five minutes with this little scrap in Mrs Peggram's kitchen, and my mind was full of questions to which I had no answers. Mrs Peggram had no answers either. It was clear, too, that she had fewer facilities than we had to look after the baby. Obviously someone had to care for him, so I offered to take him. We coaxed him into Mrs Peggram's 'moses' basket without injury to him or ourselves, tied a net on top, and put him on the back seat of my car.

For the first ten minutes of the drive home he cried pitifully, then he became silent. He's gone, I thought, I should have left him where he was, overnight, to rest. The shock of picking him up again and carrying him about must have been too much for him, but there was nothing I could have done for him at the roadside so I pressed on home.

Jean was on the doorstep.

'Have you got him?' she asked.

'Yes.' I said, and I was just going to add 'But I think he's dead', when I detected faint breathing.

'He's in a hell of a state, though,' I said, 'We'll have to get him to the vet.'

We have a vet in a million. Our efforts to treat sick wild creatures would have got nowhere without him. His name is Tom Herbert, and he lives and practises at Aberaeron, about six miles from our farm near New Quay, in Dyfed. I had first run into him shortly after the episode with the baby seal with the red mark.

'I nearly had an interesting patient for you the other night,' I told him.

'What was that?' he asked.

'A baby seal.'

'What was wrong with it?'

'As it turned out, nothing,' I said, 'but we'd been told it was injured.'

'God save us all,' said Tom, 'How am I supposed to treat baby seals?'

'I don't know,' I said, 'That's why I was going to bring it to you.'

'Oh,' he said, then after a pause, 'Is this sort of thing likely to happen often?'

'Er, yes, I think so.'

Upon which he joined the Zoological Veterinary Society, the better to help us.

He received us and our seal at eleven at night as if it was eleven in the morning. He diagnosed lung congestion and digestive discord and injected accordingly, leaving us with a bottle of Penetrane for the wounds and his assurance of total support, unsocial hours notwithstanding. We have become used to his total support since then but that was the first time we had actually met it, and the experience was like that of a pilgrim seeing Heaven's gate standing open.

When we got home we took thorough stock of our new acquisition. We counted fifty cuts on him, all septic, some of them a couple of inches long. I've no idea how they got there; they were nothing like dog bites nor the kind of wounds which might have resulted from being bashed on sharp rocks by a rough sea. His breathing was laboured and his mouth was full of pus and mucus, which explained his ghastly breath. He'd been treated for these conditions, for the time being anyway, so the main problem now was one of dehydration. We had to get some fluid into our baby, quickly, if he was to survive. We tried a baby's bottle, with Complan and glucose in it, but he wouldn't accept the teat. In fact he bit the end off it. We put some of the mixture in a hypodermic without a needle, hoping we could squirt some liquid into him, but that failed, too, because a seal's teeth are too uniform to get anything between them and he would only open his mouth to snap. We abandoned the syringe when he bit the end off it, and began to think we might have to give up altogether when, not content with teats and syringes, he bit the tip off my right index finger. He had obviously had a very rough time when he had been on the beach, from people as well as dogs, and no doubt he regarded our efforts as a continuation of the attack. Although he was resisting us as well as he could, our hearts warmed to him in his plight; misguided though his efforts were, we felt we couldn't let him down. So we tried the bottle again, and in the end he took hold of a teat without biting the end off. We never saw him swallow, and a lot of milk ran onto the floor, but quite a lot more must have run into his stomach. We wrapped him in a blanket and put him to bed in a box, three feet long, with an infra-red lamp to keep him warm. Then we went to bed ourselves, with some, though not much, hope of his survival.

It's my normal practice, in the morning, to pop down while the kettle is boiling to see how the latest patients in our Bird Hospital are doing. I had to take a firm grip on myself to do it the next morning, because I never thought that our baby seal would have survived the night. He had, though. He was sitting up in his box yelling his head off. We ate breakfast as if we'd won the pools.

Now we had to decide what to call him. It was easy. He'd come up in a moses basket so Moses he should be. It suited him extremely well, too, because his constant cry, if committed to print, could only be expressed as 'MO – O – O – O'. To this day I can't see a seal without wanting to call, 'Hello – O – O – O MO – O – O'.

Grey seals weigh between twenty-five and thirty pounds at birth and are fed by their mothers for fifteen to eighteen days, during which time their weight goes up to ninety pounds or thereabouts. Birds are programmed to fly, but are taught by their mothers what to eat and where to find it. Seals, on the other hand, are programmed to swim but their mothers desert them once their milk feeding is over, and they have to find out for themselves what to feed on. A clutch of babies together will manage to do so, though they will lose anything up to half their weight while they learn, but a solitary one will never learn to feed on his own. Moses weighed only twenty-eight pounds, although he was between three and four weeks old, and he obviously hadn't learned to eat fish yet. So he'd probably never seen one, and wouldn't have recognized one as food if he had. As his foster parents it was now up to us to wean him onto fish.

Jean spent all day with him, either throwing fish to him or drawing fish past him with a piece of cotton, but though he did, occasionally, snap, thereby chopping a fish into pieces, he made no attempt to swallow. That evening, very reluctantly, we went back to the baby's bottle treatment, to get some kind of nourishment into him. A seal's milk is 57% fat, ten times as rich as cows' milk, and there is no way of copying it, but we tried cows' milk, goats' milk, Complan, glucose, liquidized fish and cod liver oil together, separately, and in combination to keep him alive until the moment when he would eat fish.

At the end of a week, he was no more interested in fish than he had been when we started, and he had lost a pound in weight. We decided to ring Ken Jones for advice. 'You'll have to force-feed him,' he said. 'He'll die for certain if you don't.'

Well, it seemed a reasonable prospect. We were regularly force-feeding birds, and we had often had to open our dog's mouth to give her a pill, so we tried the same technique on Moses, only to find there are fundamental differences between birds, dogs and seals. First of all, no bird is so strong that you can't hold it still, and no bird will hurt you through gloves. Your own dog trusts you and will let you handle him. Moses, however, snapped viciously at anything that came near enough, and was able to inflict a lot of damage through even my hedging gloves. I couldn't get hold of his head at all, let alone get his mouth open. We tried a timber gag but that was useless because once any gag was in position there was no way of getting a fish past it. After about an hour we realized that we were getting nowhere so we rang Ken Jones again with the big question – 'How?' To our dismay he said the method varied so much between one seal and another that there was little he could say over the telephone to help.

By about ten o'clock, that is after four hours, we began to feel that we were trying to do something that really was impossible. Many people had told us that there was no way of saving orphaned baby seals, and that they all died in the end. Yet Ken Jones seemed to be able to do it, and all the seals he referred to in his book had taken fish quite readily when offered or thrown to them. Ken Jones had never failed. Had we got a real rogue, with whom it really was impossible?

Over a cup of tea we considered the choices. We couldn't possibly release Moses, to take his chance in the sea. He had no chance. With no blubber he had no insulation and no fat reserve, so if his lung congestion didn't kill him hypothermia and its consequences would. Yet if he didn't eat fish, he would slowly starve, and the prospect of watching him do that was too appalling to contemplate. Get the vet to put him down? Tom Herbert wouldn't put him down, unless he absolutely had to, and then it would break his heart to do it. Get the stuff and put him down myself? I couldn't face it either. There was no alternative. On went the hedging gloves for another attempt.

I tried a different approach this time, and found a way of holding Moses' jaws, one in each hand, so that I had control of him, while Jean tried to give him a fish. Then we ran into more trouble. Force feeding birds is relatively easy, by reason of their enormous gape. A gannet's throat looks like the Mersey tunnel and you can pop a fish down it like posting a letter. A seal, though, doesn't naturally drink, and squeezes its food between its tongue and the roof of its mouth to avoid swallowing half the Atlantic every time it eats a fish. In consequence, you have to push your fish, against considerable resistance, until the thickest part is past the constriction. This calls for a perfectly fresh, firm, fish, or it will either buckle or burst, and a certain amount of fortitude, too, because your hand will be in the seal's mouth almost to the wrist before you can let go of the fish. At the critical moment the fish shoots away like a wet orange pip. I found I had to keep my arms bent holding Moses, otherwise, when I let him go, he would whip round and get in a crafty nip between wrist and elbow. Our son, Hugh, still has a beautiful scar on his forearm, a present from Moses.

We discovered all this, by degrees, as Hugh and I took turns to hold him and Jean tried to feed him. Finally, at two o'clock in the morning, down went a herring. We put Mo in his box, wrapped him in his blanket and put his lamp on. He was asleep before we left the room. He must have been as exhausted as we were.

In the morning he was in fine fettle, yelling his head off. Clearly, although the herring was entirely foreign to his insides, it had not upset him. Even so, he did not appear to be any more interested in fish than before, and Jean had to spend another day trying hard to tempt him to eat one. His views were understandable, because even if the herring he had swallowed had brought him any pleasure there was no way he yet associated it with the fish being drawn past his nose, and no doubt he also thought the fearful battle of the previous night wasn't worth it as a necessary precursor to the delight of having a fish inside him. Fish he had to have, though, so that evening, when I got home from work, we got down to battle again. We had learned a lot the previous time, and now we managed to push a couple of fish down his throat without taking too long about it and without much loss of blood – my blood, that is. Before going to bed we succeeded in getting two more fish down.

For the rest of that week, we gave Moses three or four forced meals daily, each time giving him as many fish as he would take before he became too angry to hold. His weight went up ten pounds, his cuts largely healed, his mouth became clean. His breath was sweeter and more regular, and he looked just a bit more rounded, so we decided to risk letting him have a swim. Our bird room tank is only six feet by three feet by a foot deep, and after a good deal of reluctance at first he paddled round it and rolled over a few times. After these two weeks with us he was absolutely filthy, and we tried to help him clean up. Very swiftly, however, we came to realize that the only safe thing to use was a soft broom – everything else was too risky – and between his efforts and ours we got an enormous amount of dirt off him. After twenty minutes we took him out, because although his lungs were much better he still had no real insulation and a long stay in the cold water could well have set him back very badly. We towelled him down and got him back under his lamp. By the following evening, it was obvious that his little swim had not hurt him so we decided to let him swim for half an hour or so every evening.

During the third week, I felt that I had begun to master the art of holding Moses to feed him. I had acquired better gloves, and I was getting used to his tricks, so he connected less often with his teeth and did less damage when he did. Until one day when I couldn't hold him at all. He thrashed about and snapped really savagely. My gloves felt like cotton and even if they saved my skin I felt I had jammed my hand in a car door. I couldn't hold him anything like still enough for Jean to push a fish down him. Now that he was much bigger and stronger, he had obviously decided that he would no longer put up with the indignity of being force-fed. We tried again after an hour or so, with exactly the same result.

Then Hugh offered to try, and, to our amazement, Moses accepted him calmly, and down went his four or five mackerel quite easily. Hugh kept this up until, after about four days, Moses would have none of him either. I took over again, to be received with reason if not joy. This pattern continued for four weeks or so, during which, every four days, I would say 'your turn, son,' and four days later, Hugh would say, 'Your turn, Dad.'

We must have given Moses between twelve and twenty mackerel or herring every day. The fish went down whole, so it was easy to lace them with vitamins or any other dope we wanted, and he put on weight by leaps and bounds. In fact we lost track of his weight after it reached fifty pounds, because the performance required to weigh him became so great that, so long as he seemed fit, we didn't bother. We checked with Ken Jones, who said that six weeks or so of force-feeding was unusual but not unheard of, and congratulated us on having cut our teeth so successfully on what was clearly a very difficult baby. Our next ones, he said, would seem much easier to handle. Next ones! We were prepared to rehabilitate Mo if it killed us, but the prospect of doing this to baby seals every winter in future was unnerving.

In the seventh week Mo ate a sprat by himself. Jean was, as usual, spending an hour or two pulling fish past his nose, in the tank, using very thin nylon, when he took one, bit the middle out of it, and swallowed. He took a few more, then ate the middle out of some of those already lying in the tank. Victory, no less, for Ken said Mo would eat his own in the end. As we celebrated over wine at supper, we looked back on the six weeks with great relief, sure that the treatment was now over.

This idyllic state of affairs went on for a further week, during which we used to watch him playing happily in his tank and eating sprats – not very many but enough to keep his weight up. Then one day he went off his food altogether and began to have difficulty in breathing. We got him out of the tank and put him to bed under his lamp. By this time, he used to arrange his blanket to his own satisfaction, but that night he just lay feebly on top of it. He was no better in the morning, and Tom Herbert came over early, to give him a massive penicillin injection to fix the lung congestion which had struck again. He got steadily worse during the day, and when I came home from the office Jean was in despair. We rang Tom again but his partner was ill and he had a full evening's calls fixed already. He thought that Mo might have become allergic to penicillin and recommended an injection to counter this, a massive dose of Vitamin B12, and another antibiotic. He would leave the stuff and a syringe for us to collect.

Giving injections to an animal with a layer of blubber under the skin is difficult. You must get your injection through the blubber, but if you overestimate the thickness of the fat you may pump your dose into an organ which will be harmed by it. Giving the dose to Moses was terrifying. I held his head, Jean held his tail, Hugh gave the three injections. Mo strenuously resisted the whole proceedings and it was something of a miracle that we didn't break the needle. With no experience of giving injections to seals we were worried whether the dose was properly delivered into the shoulder muscle or was sitting in the blubber. Jean wanted to sit up with him all night but I persuaded her to come to bed. We had no evidence that human company brought Mo any pleasure, and there was no other treatment we could now offer whatever happened. We had either done the right thing, or we hadn't.

Predictably I was again afraid to go down the next morning, but Mo was still with us. It was much later than usual when he got out of his bed and slowly and lethargically he flopped around the floor. He didn't go into his tank, and didn't eat. He didn't eat the next day either, and seemed actually to have shrunk, so, with extreme reluctance, we went back to the force-feeding. We took turns again, Hugh and I, in holding him, and this went on for another five days. Finally he again ate a sprat; that is, he picked one up with his lips, transferred it an inch or two back in his mouth, bit off the head and tail in one action, and swallowed the middle bit. Then he moved on to another one, which he treated in the same way. Methodically, he demolished sprat after sprat in this way while we frantically thawed out more for him, and prayed that this miracle should not cease. He ate about half a stone in a hour, got out of his tank, went to his bed, rolled up his blanket, put his head on it, and went to sleep. We drank another bottle of wine, and went to bed ourselves.

After that relapse and recovery, Mo began to show his character. He soon made it clear that some visitors were his friends, some were not. For his friends he would be half out of his tank, flippers on the edge, reaching up towards them. For others he would stay submerged but for his eyes, just like a crocodile, and he wouldn't move until they'd gone.

Mo had particular reason to be grateful to Kathie Dix because she had a sister living near Milford Haven whom she visited every second Wednesday and on each occasion she brought back two hundredweight or so of frozen sprats for him. When Kathie came, Mo would reach up as high as he could, neck and flippers fully extended, while she bent down to rub noses with him. Curiously, this was quite a safe thing to do, because although he still snapped at anything which touched him behind or below his head, he now accepted something presented quietly from in front of him and just pushed on it with his nose. Kathie always wore very nice chiffon scarves and after she and Mo had rubbed noses for a few seconds his eye would drop and he would pull the scarf into the tank.

Another regular caller whom Mo loved to see was Jack Hicks. Mo would lie on his back for Jack, flippers crossed on his chest, the picture of innocence, the back of his head on the edge of the tank, right under Jack as he bent over him. Mo would slowly open his hind flippers, about the size of a man's hands, bring them together below the water and suddenly fling their contents, which must have amounted to a gallon of water, all over Jack. He got him every time.

No animal lover can resist rubbing the chest of a dog which lies on its back. The dog's action is a gesture, an invitation to caress it, and an indication of the dog's confidence that nothing but a caress will be forthcoming. Moses used to lie on his back, flippers open – all seals do – and we longed to rub his chest in the same way. But we never risked it. We knew he was just getting lined up to snap one's hand long before it actually touched him. Yet we couldn't help wondering whether he really did want to be caressed but wouldn't let the gesture be completed because of his inborn fear of man. I stroked him once with a broom handle but though he didn't resist and even held it in his flippers he showed no particular excitement. I made a minature version of the old-fashioned timber hay-rake, with four wooden tines in a head six inches long, and tried that.

He loved it. You could scratch him all day. He kept it by him wherever he went, in the tank or out of it, and every friend who came to see him was instantly given the rake, always handle end.

He now spent a lot of his time in the tank and would eat only in the water. Regrettably, he would defecate only in the water, too. In the wild it is perfectly normal and sanitary, and so his adoption of proper habits was in a way a matter for rejoicing, but in a hundred gallon tank it wasn't very sanitary and changing the water became a major occupation. He also took a perverse pleasure in fouling the water as soon as it was changed, and then he began objecting strenuously to having it changed at all. It was as though he liked it dirty. He quickly located the outlet and, as soon as water started running, he would push a sprat down it, enough to block it, and sit on top. Coaxing simply wouldn't budge him, and he became really nasty if we tried to push him away from it. When we tried to keep him away using a baker's wire basket, the kind of thing, now superseded by plastic, which holds a dozen or two loaves, Mo simply inserted a couple of claws into the mesh and threw it over his head, to hit the ceiling twelve feet away, with about as much effort as a man might use to flick a match. After that we decided that draining the tank was a two-man job, and waited until Mo was out on the floor. One of us would then play with him or keep him blocked off in a corner while the other wrestled with the plumbing. He soon spotted this ploy, and made for the tank like a rocket if he was out of it when one of us went into the room. Somehow we managed to change the water twice a day, which wasn't really often enough but the best we could do, and all in all we used 30,000 gallons of water.

On land, a seal moves by using its front flippers only, like a man lying prone pulling himself along with his elbows, and can move suprisingly quickly. Mo seemed to enjoy doing this, round and round the outside of the tank. One day, he decided that the floor was not slippery enough, except on the bit he had wetted when he got out of the tank, so he got in again and with one flipper systematically splashed water on the floor all round the tank. Then he could really get moving. Sometimes he would get in and out several times, splashing more water each time, till he had the floor the way he wanted it. I was watching him one night, when he came humping quietly up to me, a move which usually ended in careful investigation of my shoes, particularly if they were suede. He always examined suede shoes very carefully, whoever was wearing them, but that time, for no reason that we know of, he bit my left ankle, in some style, too – he left a scar nearly all the way round it. After that I used a piece of hardboard handy to keep him away.

The next day he was doing his flop around the floor when Jean decided to join in and go round in front of him. Away he went in pursuit, until Jean's cardigan caught on a nail. This is it, she thought, stuck fast, he'll have my foot off. In the event, with good manners, he stopped, a foot away from her, waited until she pulled the cardigan free and got going again, and away he went after her. Perhaps he found the chase more fun than the kill.

One night we found the bird-room light on, though we knew we hadn't put it on ourselves. The switch there is a cord-operated one, hanging from the ceiling. Mo had been up to his tricks, as I found when I caught him the next night, at dusk, pulling the end of the cord, which reached down to about two feet off the floor and which I'd never bothered to cut off. After that, we frequently watched him, at dusk, get out of the tank, hump over to the corner by the door, put the light on, and get back into the tank. He only ever pulled once, never too hard, just enough to operate the switch.

During the beginning of his stay with us, when he'd been very sick, we had closed him into his bed at night to keep warm. When he became fitter, we decided to leave him loose in the room, so that he could move around if he wanted. It wasn't altogether a wise move. One night he got a cupboard open and carried twenty-two towels, admittedly rather second-hand ones, into the tank, where he tore them into tiny shreds. There he lay, in the morning, with just his head showing out of a hundred gallons of towel soup.

Towards the end of February 1975, Moses spent less time in the water and more looking out of the windows, which reach the floor in the bird room. He went off his food to some extent but this didn't worry us since he was quite big enough by that time. He was fit, so we began thinking of getting him back where he belonged. We were strongly advised not to return him to the sea unless it was near a group of other youngsters whom he could join. He was used to eating dead fish, regularly supplied, and he might well feel that live ones, going past at twenty knots, were not for him. He would soon learn with other youngsters, who would accept him, but on his own he might lose a dangerous amount of fat before he got the idea, if he got it at all. Malcolm Cullen, the head warden of the Pembrokeshire National Park, undertook to find a suitable clutch of youngsters for him to join. We hoped they would be in a really inaccessible spot, because we had no real idea how Moses might behave after we had released him. He might not take readily to life in the wild, and, in spite of his aggressive behaviour with us, which might well have been due to the rough time he had on the beach and to our own inexpert handling, he might regard people as providers of his food. If so, he would surely come up onto a beach, with people on it, and sooner or later he would bite someone, and then there would be demands to shoot him.

People's reactions to seals do vary tremendously. For many years a big, solitary bull seal had spent a lot of time on the Llanina reef, about a mile from our house. One day, Hugh and I were fishing over the reef, spinning for bass, with the seal not far away. We were feeling rather cross because although we could see the fishes' dorsal fins we couldn't catch any, yet the seal slid off the rock now and again and always came up with a fish of five or six pounds which he ate methodically, holding it in his flippers. We were wearing only trunks and plimsolls, and we waded very slowly along a ridge in the reef to get nearer to the dorsal fins and, incidentally to the seal, until we were only thirty feet from him. By this time we were more interested in the seal than the fishing. He was so much better at it than we were and obviously we were not disturbing him at all. We could even hear his tummy rumbling.

Then a little yellow inflatable dinghy appeared, being rowed by an overdressed little man in a suit and a collar and tie, with a young girl in the back. The seal watched it coming and his attitude changed from complete relaxation to a fair degree of agitation. With fifty yards to go, he fairly jumped into the water. He was quite some seal, even for an old bull, being eight or nine feet long and two-feet-six or so thick, and the splash looked like a depth charge going off.

'What was that?' the man called out, much agitated also.

'A seal,' I said.

'It couldn't be,' he retorted, 'not here.'

'Yes,' I said, 'it's been sitting on this rock all afternoon.'

'Gracious heavens,' said the little man, 'it couldn't possibly be. Are you sure it wasn't a dog?'

I said I was quite sure.

He immediately turned his boat round with great haste and little aptitude, and when he was pointing the way he had come he fairly took off, his oars going like paddle wheels on emergency full power.

He must have been terribly frightened of seals. I've always wondered, though, in view of his reactions, what he thought of Hugh and me standing in four feet of water with, as far as he could see, nothing on, within spitting distance of what he must have considered to be a dangerous animal.

Feeling there must be many people like him, we worried how they would react to Mo if he came up onto a beach and asked for a fish.

Fortunately there are plenty of people with the opposite view. I remember a year or so after that episode, contractors were laying a deep-water sewer out-fall extending beyond the reef. They were blasting underwater and, knowing from experience how shock waves travel in water, we feared for that same big bull seal, so we went to see the divers, who were supervising the laying and jointing of the big pipes, to tell them he was there and to ask them to look after him. They were as big and tough a quartet as ever I saw in a caravan, but to our delight they assured us that they knew him well because he was with them whenever any of them were under water, and that although he got in the way sometimes and swam off with tools, their lives were the brighter for his presence. There was no way, they said, they would fire any charges unless they knew the seal was safe.

Anyway, to get back to Mo, in March of 1975 Malcolm Cullen rang to say that he had found half-a-dozen baby seals, at Martins Haven, in Pembrokeshire, a mile from where he lived, and, to our joy, as remote a spot as we could wish.This is the beach from which people sail for Skomer and Skokholm, the island bird sanctuaries just offshore, so a fair proportion of the people using the beach would be sympathetic towards wild creatures. It was sixty miles away and the problem was how to get him there, for he was far too active and mischievous to have loose in the car, and so big by now that no crate large enough to hold him comfortably would go in the car. Malcolm solved that one by bringing over a van and after Moses had inspected it thoroughly he sat in the back, propped up on one flipper, looking through the rear window. We followed in the car, thus having a grandstand view of the amazed reactions of passers-by in built-up areas.

We reached Martins Haven, and the moment of truth. If our efforts had been successful, Moses should now swim away, and return to the wild. We were assured that other seals the same age would accept him, and so he would soon be catching his own fish and eating them. He had ample reserves of fat for the time it would take him to learn the new technique. On the other hand, after captivity for five months, he could hardly have any memory of life in the sea, which he had left as an unweaned and sick little pup. He had been a most finicky eater, too, a fact which hardly comforted us. He had refused herring, mackerel and whiting, and had eaten nothing but sprats, except when we were force-feeding him, and then he had never touched an imperfect one – a few scales missing or a damaged fin and he wouldn't eat it. Mo's return to the sea would be like a man who never ate anything but smoked salmon finding himself in the army.

Once a seal has lost its white coat at three weeks, there is no way of marking it, so that it can easily be recognized. There are various methods of tagging the webs of the hind flippers but since seals out of water have their hind flippers closed except when stretching, the tag cannot usually be seen and certainly it is not possible to get near enough to a live seal to read the number on its tag. Moses's most distinctive mark was a round scar, about an inch across, halfway up his nose, so we issued portraits of him to anyone who might be interested, showing the scar.

We had to carry him in a blanket over some rough ground to get him to the beach, and we set him down about thirty feet from the sea. His eyes seemed to open to double their normal size as he stared at it. Then he flopped steadily into the water. He paused to look at a rock with seaweed on it, dealt with a couple of little waves, a foot or so high, and swam out to about five feet of water. He had never been in more than a foot of water before and his first couple of dives were hilarious. Instead of porpoising like seals normally do, he stood on his head with his back end right out of the water, and then slowly sank. When he came up he shot halfway out of the water and stood, treading water, with his front flippers in a 'hands up' position. For ten minutes we saw his head from time to time while he investigated one side of the bay, then we lost sight of him.

We went off to have tea with Malcolm and his family but our minds were still on the beach, and when we left Jean said, 'Let's go back and have a last look.'

'What if he's on the beach?' I said. 'We can't do anything for him now, whatever happens.'

'I'd just like to make sure,' said Jean, so down we went. Praise be, there was no sign of him.

The house felt very empty when we got back to it. It was as if we had just lost a pet dog. After a few days, Malcolm said Mo hadn't come up on the beach or been seen, so we began to feel hopeful. We reflected that he must have been a born survivor to have got over the condition he was in when we first had him, so that a little thing like a complete change of lifestyle wouldn't bother him for long. Anyway, we'd given him a second chance, and now it was up to him.

In July, we got a card from John Davies, the warden of Skomer bird sanctuary, to say that when he and his wife, Hazel, had gone for a swim the previous Sunday, Mo had come up and swum with them. John had been to see Mo several times when he was with us, so he really knew him, scar and all, and was quite certain of the identification. Mo was as fat as butter, he assured us, and as far as he could see was perfectly fit. That meant that, after three months on his own, he must have been fully rehabilitated and was now ready to play his part in the world.

The card arrived on our wedding anniversary. It made our day.

2

Laying the Foundations

I was brought up by parents whose interests never included wild life. They would travel to see historic buildings or lovely scenery, but were quite unconcerned about anything alive unless it had clothes on – and was decently Methodist. Just where my interest in birds originated remains one of the mysteries of my life but I know it was there from an early age, even if it lay dormant for a long time. I well remember at school, when I once mistook the call of a wood pigeon for that of an owl, not only how amazed was the one boy who knew better, but how much more amazed were the other boys that anyone should care.

I soldiered in the Far East during the Second World War, where the birds are bigger, brighter and more numerous than they are in Britain, and I began to take notice of them. Several of us used to make a bee-line for a book shop whenever we got into a town, but we could find very few suitable books on birds. When at last I sailed home I was able to identify only vultures, peafowl and a raptor properly called a kite hawk but, by reason of its unsavoury eating habits, usually called something else, unless ladies were present.

Jean and I met and married in 1949 and set up house in Cardiff, where I was building bridges and roads for the County of Glamorgan. This was a rewarding enough activity if the schemes got beyond the drawing stage and took physical shape on the ground, but extreme stringency was the watchword in the matter of highway funds and very few of them did. We started taking our precious fortnight's holiday in Pembrokeshire and immediately fell in love with that most beautiful county. We bought a little caravan so as to go there more often (and more cheaply) and soon found we were spending a dozen or more weekends down there each summer, as well as our regular fortnight's holiday. It was there that our joint interest in birds really developed.

One summer fortnight, before we bought the caravan, a Wing Commander Scourfield was staying in the same pub as ourselves, the *Ship*, in Solva. Although he was a naturalist of note, he never pushed his interest on others, but one evening, as we strolled with him along the cliffs, he began talking about the enormous variety of seabirds we could see. Our ignorance on the subject was abysmal. We knew so little about the behaviour of the birds, and could not identify more than half of the species in sight, but the Wing Commander's enthusiasm was infectious and we listened intently to every word he said. His knowledge of the birds was immense but it was the obvious joy and pleasure he derived from watching them that made the greatest impression on us. He clearly regarded the birds as part of his life, of his heritage as a citizen of this country. We began to appreciate that the same pleasure was available to us, too, given the necessary knowledge, and we have been acquiring that ever since.

Life in Cardiff soon became very frustrating. Fewer and fewer road schemes seemed to be carried out. The only one that remains in my mind from that time was a case in which the obvious line of a widening involved the felling of a regular avenue of lovely Scots pines, really big ones. I produced a scheme which took the road the other side of them altogether and contrived to make it appear less costly than felling and uprooting the trees. It worked, surprisingly, and the trees are still there, twenty-five years later, in a neat banana-shaped island. We were horribly broke, too, and kept all the cash we could to go west as often as possible in the summer. Because those were the days of working on Saturday mornings we could only go at most every second week. We got to dread a fine weekend in the summer.

Our final disenchantment with urban life came when a pair of tawny owls set up home in a beautiful beech tree just by our house in Cardiff. We were absolutely thrilled and watched them every evening. Their hooting was a lullaby, far more soothing than the noise from traffic and other city sounds. We were, therefore, appalled to be asked to sign a petition calling on the City Council to get rid of the owls either by shooting them or by felling the tree. We were even more shattered when we failed to get any significant support for a counter-petition, and though nothing actually happened to the owls or the tree while we were there, we lived in a state of considerable tension for a long time.

We decided, one day, that we had simply had enough. We knew by now that we wanted to live in a rural setting, not an urban one, by the sea if at all possible, but in the country anyway. 'If we are not to build any roads,' I said to Jean, 'let's go and not build roads by the sea.'

In 1957 I took over the maintenance of the roads of the southern half of what was then the County of Cardigan, a very different matter from drawing plans of schemes which were never done. No one can look after six hundred miles of road without spending much of his time looking at them. I must admit that I used to look at the one passing the local heronry and the one passing the lake with the great crested grebes on it rather more often than strict rotation required. The good people of one parish once expressed their appreciation of the frequency with which I had been inspecting their roads, but I never told them that I had one day spotted a goshawk on a tree by their village and kept returning to photograph it. Unexpectedly perhaps, my work and my wild life interests have never clashed. I have always been able to programme the grubbing up of hedges at a time outside the nesting season, and to arrange the repair of old stone bridges at a time when dippers are not bringing up their families in the holes in the masonry the programmed repairs are intended to fill.

We found and bought a small holding about a mile outside New Quay, called Penfoel. Pen, in Welsh, means head, or top, and a foel is a bare or windswept hill. It isn't particularly bare now, though it must have been so originally. 'Night on the Bare Mountain' is our signature tune, though in fact there are some nice ash and sycamore trees on the property, with tawny owls living in many of them. Apart from a decent little barn, the only building on the property was a tripartite one, comprising cart-shed, cottage, and cowshed. Here we had our first pang of conscience as conservationists. The cartshed and cowshed were roofed in slate but the cottage roof was tin sheet covering rotten thatch, in which there were a lot of rats and a pair of barn owls. We knew we couldn't retain the latter and get rid of the former so we simply stripped the lot, built a new first-floor, turned the cartshed into the dining room, and in due course, many years later, the cowshed became the bird hospital, or at least its intensive care unit.

Now that we lived by the sea, we spent a lot of time walking the beaches, as well as wandering about the lovely countryside all around us. Anyone who does this will find the odd bird which seems to be in need of care and attention, and we used to bring home any we found so that we could try to save them. When our children, Hugh and Diana, walked to the village school they used to find sick birds in the half-mile of heavily hedged road which separated the two places, and they would bring them home. The other children got to know about this, of course, so before long any bird found in trouble anywhere near us used to be brought to Penfoel.

The only thing one knows about a 'patient' is that it can't fly, and if examination shows no broken bones the cause of the bird's trouble might be almost anything – impact, attack by a predator, disease, poison. There is no time for proper diagnosis. An illness which will take months to kill a human will kill a bird in as many hours. One can be sure of two things – any bird which can't fly will be in a state of shock and probably badly dehydrated, so one must first give it glucose and water, forcibly if necessary, and then let it rest. There is very little doubt that nature, the Good Lord and the natural toughness of the little fellows had more to do with our recovery figures in the early days than anything we actually did by way of treatment, but we learned the value of glucose solution, rest and warmth, and surprisingly often the afternoon's huddled little bundle became the morning's sleek and lively bird, fighting to be off.

We soon learned to appreciate that, when treating wild birds, they must feel terrified at being handled. One is so anxious to help that the bird's own feelings are easily over-looked, but it seems reasonable to suppose that a bird, being handled, must feel much as you or I would feel being handled by a benevolent dinosaur. You would be much relieved, each time it put you down, that it had not pulled your arms and legs off, but you would greatly fear it was going to, each time it picked you up.

Any bird treatment unit will always have baby birds brought to it in the appropriate season and a number of fledglings were among those first birds we treated. This is the most contentious part of the work of a bird hospital, the one aspect where it can be argued that harm is being done, because the chances of a hand-reared bird establishing itself in the wild are very remote. Babies of some species take food quite readily from one's fingers or from forceps and soon eat on their own. Others have to be fed constantly, but, given enormous patience, and a delicate enough touch, most birds can be kept going until they have their full plumage and can be released. Unless there is something seriously wrong with it, any bird will fly once its feathers are fully grown and obviously one puts a bird in a decent-sized aviary to make sure, but there is no way in which a human foster-parent can teach a baby bird, as its own parents would, what it should eat, how it should live, and that it must keep away from cats. Unless a newly-released bird can find its own food within a few hours it will not survive, and it is arguable that if a bird is to die, it is better for this to happen when it is a fledgling than later, when its senses are fully developed. It is also argued that the existence of a unit prepared to take in baby birds and try to fledge them encourages people to pick up apparently lost 'youngsters' which would be much better left alone.

We learned all this the hard way. Jean is chief feeder of fledglings, and she used to treat each baby as if it were human and heir to the throne. She would get up at first light to feed them, because their own parents would start at that time and she felt that the interval between first light, in June, and seven o'clock or so, was too long to leave them. Swifts, to give an example, will only take minute quantities at a time so they have to be fed every half-hour or so. Keeping half-a-dozen swifts going is a full-time job for one person. After innumerable disappointments Jean still adopts these habits, but we both feel that in trying to bring up baby birds we are on a hiding to nothing. Strangely, people who bring in oiled or injured birds apologize profusely for the trouble they are inflicting on us, are most appreciative of what we are going to do and contribute to the funds, but people who bring in fledglings, which are going to be far more trouble still seem to think that they are doing us a favour.

One day Jean went to meet Hugh and Diana from school and found them terribly upset. During afternoon playtime, they said, they had spotted three tawny owls, too young to fly, in the field alongside the school, and a cat stalking them. The head teacher had refused point-blank to let the children go to get them, so Jean found herself appointed rescuer-in-chief and everyone went off to find the owls. Only one was still there, and was brought home very proudly, wrapped in a yellow duster. Owls have a disconcerting trick of pretending to be dead which leads one, naturally, to relax one's grip. Relax too much, though, and your owl will be over the hedge in no time. Fortunately we knew that trick and held on to ours.

Having felt guilty on behalf of the entire human race over the treatment of the owls in Cardiff, we were doubly bound to save this one. He was a beautiful creature, though pitifully thin, and we dreamed of ultimately releasing him, fit and fat, to take his place in our little world where no one would shoot him or cut his tree down. We gave him, and he accepted, prodigious amounts of meat, suitably wrapped in Labrador hair for roughage, and we quite convinced ourselves that he was looking better every day. Nagging doubts arose, though, when we picked him up, because though he looked fine he wasn't getting any fatter. We pushed the doubts aside. Give him time, we said. We put him in the spare bedroom, where he spent most of the time in a box; on the door handle outside a sign said 'Please keep closed. Owl loose.'

He only lasted a week, and, since the Nature Conservancy Council was asking for the bodies of any dead birds of prey, we sent him off for a post-mortem. We learned that he was so badly infested with worms that he had starved to death. We felt that the debt of *homo sapiens* to the genus owl had increased.

We might have carried on in the same haphazard way for ever, but not long afterwards a much more significant patient arrived for treatment. David Jenkins, a friend of ours, was motoring home one night and found a buzzard lying in the road. It was very nearly dead, but David and his wife sat with it for most of the night, giving it chopped egg and tiny drops of brandy. They kept this up the next day, but felt the buzzard was well enough to leave alone the second night. They fed him all the second day, but since they were both working, they decided they could not possibly look after him properly and asked us to have him.

After robins, blackbirds and one baby owl, a buzzard was a real challenge, so we took him in. He was far bigger than anything we had handled before. A buzzard can easily kill a rabbit with his talons, and dismember one with his beak. A close examination of that organ suggested that we had better be careful with our fingers. A buzzard's eyes are set wide apart to help him judge distance accurately in front of him, typical of a predator; a buzzard does not have to worry about what lies behind him. His eyes are deepset under enormous beetling eyebrows, and they solemnly watch you if you are anywhere near him. One of Jean's magazines that week had in it a list of names and their interpretations, and therein we found that 'Duncan' meant 'Brown Chieftain'. That description so perfectly suited our buzzard that we joyfully called him Duncan right from first acquaintance.

When we came to handle Duncan he seemed completely paralysed. His wings and legs were locked in fixed positions and his talons were closed up tight. We had to open his beak to feed him, although he was able to swallow by himself. The problem. of diagnosis arose, as it always does. He might have eaten a poisoned rat, or mole, or suffered brain damage from being hit by a car. Yet there was no sign of impact damage. Equally, paralysis was not normally the result of poisoning with strychnine, as used on moles, or warfarin, as used on rats. We fed him with raw meat, as much as he would eat, and gave him a five day course of antibiotics, a daily multi-vitamin capsule and an occasional iron tonic tablet. No one we knew, not even Tom Herbert, could suggest anything else.

As his talons were locked, he was unable to perch, so he was fouling his own tail badly, and his droppings hardened like concrete. So we made a perch which he could straddle. This kept his plumage clean and gave him a chance to move his legs. On the third day we found him off his perch, so some part of him had obviously started to work again.

At the end of a week he could move his wings and his right leg. Jean made a sling from a pair of nylon briefs to support him and after two weeks he was able to pick up sticks in his right claw. David Jenkins called in to see him and Duncan, with a prodigious effort, flopped about twelve feet along the floor, finishing up exhausted and panting at his feet.

Any land bird will be frightened of people for a week or two after capture. Some never become used to people and show obvious fright if approached. Duncan, however, lost all fear of us after about two weeks, so we decided to take him with us about the house. When we finally sat down in the evening, Duncan sat on my right knee, on a towel, on the right hand end of the settee. Honey, our labrador bitch, occupied the rest of the settee and always laid her head on my left knee. Neither took the slightest notice of the other.

After about an hour, Duncan started to vibrate all over and we thought he was having some kind of fit. Jean said 'I wonder if he wants to splatt'. I held him over the coal scuttle, the nearest reasonably convenient spot, and sure enough he relieved himself on the instant. Incredibly, that buzzard was house-trained. He never once made a mess on anyone or in the wrong place. He used to start his vibrating act in plenty of time for us to get him over the scuttle or the kitchen sink or outside altogether.

He gradually got better until after six or seven weeks he would flap his wings, not powerfully enough to fly but well enough to get about quite rapidly. His talons were now strong enough for him to perch properly. A tame buzzard was unusual enough for many people to come from far and near to see him. Some farmers held the view that buzzards, like crows, peck the eyes out of new born lambs, but the sight of Duncan, perhaps because he was such a handsome bird, convinced them the old wives' tale was wrong. Why it should have done so we never could understand but it was a good thing that it did.

Yet after eight weeks, Duncan died. We were sure his death was not related to the original complaint, whatever that was, but we were not consoled for a long while. Not for the first time, and certainly not the last, we wondered what good we were doing. Had Duncan suffered during the weeks we were trying to help him? Possibly it would have been kinder to put him down at the beginning, but unless someone, somewhere, tried to save sick birds no one would ever find out how to do so, and though there would undoubtedly be cases where painless death was the kindest treatment only experience would tell us which those cases were.

We had had Duncan for fifty-six days and for fifty-four of them he had been getting better, and we had both talked about him with others a good deal, far more than we had about any bird we had treated before. People over a much wider area now knew that we were willing to treat sick birds and, considering that we had in fact failed to save Duncan, they had an entirely unfounded impression that we were good at it. It was a good case of high marks for trying, but on the strength of our efforts over Duncan, Jean was asked to be the Auxiliary Secretary for New Quay for the RSPCA.

In each town or district the RSPCA has a uniformed inspector who is the official representative of the Society in all matters. For instance, he organizes the rescue of sheep from cliffs and dogs from mine shafts, and brings prosecutions in known cases of cruelty. He is supported by a branch committee comprising an auxiliary secretary for each village or suburb or whatever, a few general executive members, and the usual officials. The committee members, particularly the auxiliary secretaries, raise funds, find homes for stray or unwanted dogs and cats, and keep an ear to the ground for things to report to the Inspector. Given a good committee and a good inspector, a branch can do wonders, and we had a grand outfit. The Chairman was a retired General, Lewis Pugh, who had lost none of his powers of leadership and, though he often asked more of his committee, to which I was duly co-opted, than flesh and blood and other commitments would allow, we never left a meeting without a burning desire to do great things. Our Inspector, Bill Hallam, was in a class of his own, being totally devoted to the Society and the cause it served. He could not have done more than he did for animal welfare without giving up eating and sleeping. He believed in persuasion, not prosecution, in looking after the Society's affairs, since in his mind a prosecution indicated that cruelty *had* taken place and, therefore, that he had failed in his job. He was universally liked and respected, not least by those with whom he had remonstrated over some act he considered less than humane.

Bill was not a vet and did not profess or try to be one, but he had an immense store of practical knowledge which he loved to impart. He knew how to hold a bird without hurting it, or letting it hurt the holder: he knew how to feed it, and with what. 'Scrambled egg will keep any bird going for days', he would say, 'but always make it with water, not milk. Milk gives them the runs.' RSPCA Inpsectors are not given any facilities to hold or treat sick birds or animals but Bill Hallam was laughing where birds were concerned. He brought all his to us.

We talked a great deal with him about sick and injured birds and learnt much thereby, but above all we talked of oiled sea birds. Bill had dealt with lightly oiled birds from the docks at Southampton, but, living on the coast, and acutely aware of the results of the Torrey Canyon disaster, we were sure that sooner or later some badly oiled birds would turn up. There was at that time no known effective way of getting the oil off a badly-contaminated sea bird so that it would regain its waterproof properties and return to the wild.

I well remember that our life changed at about half-past five one Friday in February 1971, when a man arrived on our doorstep with two guillemots, liberally coated in oil, saying that there were more on the beach, in the same state. We went down, and found four more before it got dark. Hugh and some of his friends searched all day Saturday but there were no more to be seen.

Nothing we had read about the Torrey Canyon disaster or oiled birds elsewhere had prepared us for the real thing. The six birds we had were all guillemots, though it was not easy to tell. A guillemot is normally a pert, perky little bird, with a white breast and brown-black wings, back and tail, and an upright stance like a small penguin. These birds were lying on their breasts, which were black, and were holding their wings away from their bodies, dragging them on the ground as if they were too heavy to hold up. Their eyes were lack-lustre, their beaks were covered in oil, inside and out. Obviously they had in-gested oil which now rotting away their insides. A badly-oiled bird is a heart-rending sight. News pictures, however good, never fully convey their dejection and total helplessness. I'm sure that if more people actually saw oiled birds before treatment, the resulting outcry would bring some action to stop the pollution which causes all the trouble.

We felt pretty helpless ourselves in the presence of these guillemots. The birds looked so much worse than we had imagined that we were desperate for help. Bill was twenty-five miles away, the postal strike was on, and, not being on STD, we couldn't telephone him. We phoned the police, though, who are always tremendously helpful, and, with their own ways of doing these things, they got hold of Bill for us and he came down on the Saturday morning. By then two of the birds were dead. We had them in a pen in the barn, following Bill Hallam's instructions to keep them out of draughts but at normal air temperature.

It was universally believed in those days that a water bird's plumage was waterproof because of the presence on it of oils, secreted by a gland near the tail and spread over the feathers in the course of preening. If this oil was washed off with the contaminant, the waterproof properties were lost, apparently for good, so the use of solvents or detergents was out. The accepted routine was to sprinkle the bird with fullers earth which would absorb the oil and form a mixture which would break up and come off in water. We sprinkled liberally, though without very much real hope. Indeed, two more died that Saturday.

The two survivors began to look just a little more perky on Sunday, so we called them Pip and Squeak. The fullers earth was clearly doing something, since the build-up of oil/dust mixture was becoming obvious. Monday came, and our spirits began to lift: by tea time when I came home, our birds were walking about, absolutely filthy dirty, but very very much better than they had been when they arrived.

It was too good to last. On Tuesday morning, Squeak was dead, and Pip was standing sadly by the body. We knew about the disastrous survival rate of birds oiled by the Torrey Canyon, but we had really begun to have hopes for these two. We thought we knew exactly how Sisyphus must have felt each time he got his rock to the top of his hill and watched it run down again. At this point, Jean started doing things her way.

'Pip'll be lonely out here in the barn on his own,' she said. 'And he'll be fighting the cold all the time. I'm going to bring him in.'

So in he came, and took up residence in an orange crate in the kitchen. When I came home on Wednesday he was out of his crate, cuddled up to the Rayburn, and his dish of sprats was in front of him. Honey, the labrador, had been properly introduced to him, and seemed to have adopted him as part of the family. The layers of fullers earth and oil were by now very thick indeed, so we decided to try the next stage of the process. We put Pip in three inches of water in the bath, enough to let him get wet if he wanted to but not so deep that he wouldn't be able to keep his feet on the bottom.

The black muck that came off him was prodigious. Within minutes the water was opaque but, amazingly, it all went down the plug hole quite easily. We gave him a second dowsing and that seemed to do the trick. We mopped him down, and let him dry off by the fire. He had seemed to enjoy himself so much in the water that a pattern was set which was to be followed for three weeks. Each evening we'd take Pip up to the bath, dry him off, sprinkle him with fullers earth again, and repeat the dose. Soon he had the run of the house, and, apart from the need for an occasional lick with a damp cloth, he never gave any trouble. He would sit quite happily with Honey, though he loved to explore every room of the ground floor of the house.

One day, when Jean was making up our bed, she heard him making a fearful noise in the kitchen. She made the bottom of the stairs in one bound and the kitchen in two, to find him squawking his head off and hammering the door of the fridge with his beak. His dish of sprats was empty.

Then one night, we realized that he had been in the bath for half an hour at least, and was still perfectly dry. We left him for another half hour to make sure, but not a feather was wetting up and we knew we'd won. We also knew we had come to the parting of the ways, because there was no reason to keep him any longer. The next fine evening, we took him to a secluded cove, near a rock where guillemots breed in the summer, and released him on the ebbing tide. He looked so small, yet although we knew it was his proper environment and although the evening was calm, the sea looked very big and hostile.

In he went, without hesitation, and started diving and shaking himself furiously. He swam steadily away, still diving and preening, and we watched him through the glasses until finally we couldn't see him at all. There was nothing more we could have done for him. He was clean, he was waterproof and he was fat as butter, but he had been a real poppet and the house felt very empty for a while without him.

But we had saved an oiled bird. Only one, granted, but the survival rate after the Torrey Canyon disaster had been below one in a hundred and we'd saved one out of six. If we'd had a hundred, maybe we would still only have saved one, but at least we had been successful. If he'd been dour, or nasty or even just uninteresting, our enthusiasm might have been reduced and our future quite different, but because he'd been none of these things we were filled with an urge to do everything we could for others like him in the future. The fact that no one really knew how to do much for oiled birds lay heavily on us, but that cloud was to be blown away in early 1972.

3

Early Birds

The Torrey Canyon disaster in 1968 stimulated research into the treatment of oiled birds and an ad hoc unit, funded by the oil companies was set up in the Zoology department of the University of Newcastle-upon-Tyne. Its work was featured in the BBC's *Tomorrow's World* programme in early 1972, which Jean and I happened by chance to be watching. The programme briefly described the unit's findings and gave an address to write to for full details. We did so on the spot, and a few days later became the proud owners of the *Recommended Treatment of Oiled Seabirds*, published by the Oiled Seabird Research and Rehabilitation Unit, at Newcastle.

Newcastle's research had found that the waterproof qualities of a water bird's plumage depended on the physical properties of the feathers. Substantially, the air spaces in a feather were so small that water, with its high surface tension, would not enter or pass through them. The slightest contamination, however, destroyed this property. Dip a breast feather from a duck or a swan into clean water or hold it under a tap and, provided it is clean in the first place, it will end up as dry and 'feathery' as it was before, save that there may be globules of water on it, exactly like the globules on a newly-waxed motor car when it first gets wet, and these will drop off when the feather is tilted over. Dip the feather in dirty water, though, and it will emerge bedraggled, all the downy, 'feathery' processes stuck together. Rinse it in hand-hot water and it will, in time, be dry again.

This explained a great deal which had previously been obscure. It killed the myth, which had bedevilled the treatment of oiled birds for years, that waterbirds were waterproof because natural oils on their plumage kept them so. The oils are there all right, though they are actually waxes, not oils, but a bird can be perfectly waterproof without them. The quantity on a bird is very small indeed, and attempts, during the early stages of the research, to waterproof birds by applying the waxes artificially failed because it wasn't possible to apply them sparingly enough. Excess natural wax turned out to be as much a contaminant as anything else.

Preening by waterbirds is a major activity, occupying most of the time they are not sleeping or actively feeding. Newcastle's research showed that the prime object of this was to service the feathers and to repair any which had become disturbed or damaged. A bird will, in seconds, completely restore a mangled feather by refixing the thousands of minute barbs which compose it, something a human couldn't do for many a month, even using a microscope.

Waterbirds' breast feathers, which are actually in the water most of the time, show these properties mostly at the tip, the rest of the feather being downy. The feathers are very closely spaced and the tips overlap like the tiles on a roof, forming a waterproof membrane, separated from the bird's body by the down, which provides the insulation necessary when it is floating on a pond or in the middle of the Atlantic in the winter. This 'membrane' is obviously a very delicate affair indeed, and requires constant attention, because a very slight disturbance will result in air spaces big enough for water to penetrate. Every feather is attended to regularly, and even a small bird has 10,000 feathers. A swan has 25,000. Once water got past the feather tips, we learned, it would spread right round the bird through the down, until it was completely waterlogged.

The failure of previous efforts to clean birds with oil on them was now explained, too. Apart from fullers earth, which was effective in only a small number of cases, there were two main cleaning media, solvents and detergents. The only solvent used to any extent had been petrol, all the others being too expensive and difficult to get. Petrol soon had a bird looking beautifully clean, but when it evaporated it left the anti-knock compounds on the bird. Newcastle found that the more effective a detergent was at removing oil, the more difficult it was to rinse off the detergent afterwards, and minute traces of detergent, or minute traces of anti-knock compounds, were quite enough to keep a bird waterlogged.

To rehabilitate an oiled bird, it was necessary to get it absolutely, chemically, physically, operating-theatre clean. The recommended medium was washing-up liquid, but it was pointed out that the best detergents for washing plates were not necessarily also the best ones for washing oiled birds. The recommended ones were all cheap ones – Co-op, Keynote, Winfield, and Alliance.

The Newcastle recommendations also stressed the importance of the medical treatment of the birds in the early stages after capture. A bird should not be washed straight away. It was essential to keep it warm, to put a little poncho on it to prevent it preening and so ingesting more oil, and to keep the birds separate to prevent them preening each other. Each bird should be dosed to help clear its gut of oil and to treat the enteritis the oil would undoubtedly have caused, given vitamins, and fed. Only when the birds had perked up and so were out of shock, could they be washed. Provided the recommendations were followed meticulously, a survival rate of better than half could be expected.

We got our chance to test the recommendations in late

1972, on Wednesday, 13th November to be exact, when quite a small oil slick appeared off the coast, and some birds started to come ashore with oil on them. By the evening we had taken charge of five guillemots. We put ponchos on them, as advised, dosed them, gave them a multi-vitamin tablet each, and fed them. A newly-captured bird won't recognize dead fish as food, so it has to be force-fed. This is most easily done by two people, one of whom holds the bird's wings while the other opens its bill and pops the fish down, but it can be done quite readily single-handed by wrapping the bird in a towel first. The actual insertion of the fish is easy provided one is careful not to trap the bird's tongue and force that down as well. Slices of white fish, finger-sized for guillemots, are better than sprats at this stage, because bones are likely to do further damage to the bird's gut, already eroded by the oil. Our guillemots sat, one each to an orange crate, in the kitchen, looking absolutely pitiful, and passing oil in their droppings.

Their arrival could not have been less opportune. I was due the next day at the Public Works Show in London, where the makers and vendors of earth-moving machinery and so on showed off their wares, and purveyors of the materials of the construction industry disseminate information and hospitality. Attendance was desirable for anyone with a job like mine and while not actually obligatory a poor view would have been taken if I had stayed away. Jean and I spent much of the evening agonizing over whether I ought to attend, but eventually we decided that since I would only be away for a couple of days, and since we were not going to do much with the birds during that time anyway, I should go.

I think the prospect of treating these birds got a bit out of proportion that night, and the thought of leaving Jean on her own for a couple of days made things worse. The Newcastle recommendations spoke of a probable recovery rate of fifty per cent or better, but while this was a far higher proportion than anyone had obtained before, it still meant that something like half the birds were going to die, in our home, in our care, and we were going to feel terrible about it. The previous year, our only experience in the matter, there had been no recognized effective way of treating the birds, so anything we achieved now would be cause for rejoicing. The immediate future was rather like a visit to the dentist, something to which one is committed but wants to get over quickly. We had really been looking forward to using the Newcastle method, but now the crunch had come we weren't very sure.

These worries were expunged temporarily later in the evening. Hugh came home at half past ten from Aberaeron Fair to find a horse, belonging to a neighbour, stuck fast in our cattle grid. Three of its legs were down between the bars and on first examination it looked as if they might all be broken. In fact, more detailed inspection showed he was suffering only from severe skin abrasion, but Tom Herbert had to anaesthetize him and some of the grid bars had to be burnt out before he could be freed. By the time we got to bed, about half-past four, the prospect of cleaning oiled guillemots had returned to normal in our minds – we couldn't wait to get at it.

I duly went to London the next morning, slept like a log all the afternoon, and woke just in time to meet some old friends. We had a magnificent dinner, went to a late show, and I went to bed feeling great. I was still feeling great when I got to Olympia the next morning.

The Show now takes place at the National Exhibition Centre in Birmingham, which of course is much bigger, but terribly cold and impersonal. Nasty little salesmen pop out from cover and try to interest you in nasty little Japanese pumps and things, and no one knows anybody. It wasn't like that in Olympia. I was pursued by people I knew, with requests like 'would you like to buy a little bulldozer for your farm'. I was mystified by this sudden interest in my little holding, let alone why or how everyone in the trade seemed to have heard about it. In the end they let me off the hook. Someone had the *Western Mail*, the South Wales paper, and on page two was a splendid picture of Jean, holding a much foreshortened and so enormous guillemot, on our kitchen table. The column spoke of vast numbers of oiled birds on the premises and referred to my better half as 'Mrs Bryant, a farmer's wife . . .'

I abandoned the show and came home on the first train I could catch. When I entered the kitchen I encountered twenty-five birds – nothing like the number the *Western Mail* had suggested, but plenty to be going on with. They had all been dumped on Jean while I was on the way up to London. Three were clean, and were loose on the floor, with a tea chest to take refuge in if they wanted, but the rest sat in their ponchos, one to an orange crate, and looked terrible. The clean ones were bright of eye, which was a good sign, and standing upright, which was another good sign, but not on their toes, which would have been a better sign still. They persisted in standing in corners, facing the wall, which worried us for a long time until we realized that in nature guillemots only come ashore to breed, which they do on narrow cliff edges. There they stand facing the cliff, away from the sea, so in studying our kitchen units they were only doing what came naturally to a guillemot with its feet on a hard surface.

While I had been on my way to London, Jean had decided to wash three birds, which were perky enough and standing upright. The job is done with a one per cent solution of washing-up liquid, which amounts to a quarter of a pint of detergent to three gallons of water. Surprisingly, a stronger solution is less, not more effective. Provided one's hands can stand it, the hotter the water the better. A bird's blood temperature is well above ours, 106° or so F, so water which feels really hot to the hands will feel only lukewarm to a bird. Hot water will get the oil off very much more quickly than cool, which reduces the strain on the bird as well as on the washer, but I must admit that, even now, when I start washing a bird I feel I am going to cook it, not clean it.

Washing an oiled bird is very much a matter of leaving everything to the detergent. Elbow grease is out, since too much agitation results in distorted and mangled feathers which will never become waterproof. The bird should be immersed in the solution up to its neck for ten seconds or so, and the plumage should then be kneaded very gently with the finger tips, and only in the direction of the lie of the feathers. After a little while the oil will begin to soften, and will soon come off in the solution.

The mess in the early stages is considerable, and it was at its height on Jean's first bird when the phone rang. She couldn't just leave the bird behind in the water or let it loose in the kitchen, so she wrapped it in an old towel and dived for the phone, rubber gloves and all. The call was from the *Western Mail*, asking for information about the oiling. Having taken the call, she was soon deep in conversation with the reporter, devoutly wishing she'd let it ring.

Cradled in her right hand, more or less on her lap, the guillemot was looking round, apparently quite happily, when without warning, it took hold of the nearest protuberance, the tip or business end of the port side hemisphere of Jean's upper vital statistic, and didn't let go. Poor Jean couldn't put the phone down because it was firmly stuck to her oily rubber glove. I never found out exactly what happened next but some of the stranger bits in the *Western Mail* column were explained, for there was oil on all four walls of the hall as well as on the ceiling. But the bird looked fine, and so did the other two Jean had washed.

As I've said, a bird can be washed single-handed, particularly given a little practice, but the disadvantage is that it can get its head into the solution, which naturally stings its eyes and it may even drink some, which won't do it any good either. With guillemots and razorbills, there is much to be said for tying up their beaks with a narrow strip of insulating tape or a very small elastic band. Apart from preventing the bird drinking, this stops it pecking at the holder. The great objection to a single-handed operation is that one's hold is not too secure, and if the bird struggles one's automatic reaction is to grip it a little tighter, which will inevitably scare it half to death. So it is better for the bird if two people do the job.

Several birds were ready, so I washed one. The oil came off quite easily, but it took two waterings before we were satisfied. Rinsing it was the next problem. This has to be done in hot water, like the washing process, so we had to use the hand-held shower in the bathroom, the only source of temperature-controlled water in the house. It is essential to spray the bird since the detergent will not come off in still water. On the contrary, detergents are surface-active, so if a nearly clean bird is put into water which has a little detergent in it, it will attract more detergent to itself. The detergent already on it will not disperse.

A bird just washed looks like a drowned rat, its breast looks like off-white felt, and when lifted out of the washing bowl an astonishing amount of water will run off it. Spraying is done against the lie of the feathers, to help penetration, and quite soon water will pearl off the bird's back in droplets, instead of soaking in. Spraying the breast will result, in time, in white patches showing up in the 'felt'. These are feathers which have been rinsed clean and have separated from the rest. In time the whole breast will be white, and water will be pearling off that, too, every feather being free.

Rinsing has to continue until all the detergent has gone. The bird should then be dry, since all the various contaminants will have been washed off. Not quite dry, of course, for the plumage will still be damp, but dry enough not to retain water. If, on picking the bird up, more than a few drops of water run off it, or if squeezing the feathers finds any water, either the washing or the rinsing has not been thorough enough. It takes at the very least half an hour to rinse a bird after washing it, quite often more than an hour, but to get a bird dry is one of the big moments in the whole operation. It is a terrible strain on the bird and it's not unusual to find him drooping a bit before the rinsing is finished. This means completing the rinsing the next day, since there is little virtue in having a dry bird if he is also dead. The real disaster is to find, after a great deal of unsuccessful rinsing, a spot of oil somewhere which has survived the washing, since this means going through the whole process again.

We got our bird, so we thought, beautifully dry, and exulted in the way the recommended process worked. We bore it triumphantly down to the kitchen and put it in a pen by the Rayburn to dry thoroughly, first treating its feet with hand cream to stop the webs drying out and cracking. We had achieved more in two hours with this bird than we had with Pip in two weeks, but it looked as though we should have to treat our birds single-handed or we would never finish. So Jean washed and I rinsed, and we had two more clean birds when we went to bed. That made six clean ones in all. And by teatime on Thursday, another six were dry.

After a bird is dry, the next stage is to let it swim in a tank of clean water. It will splash water all over itself, actively working it into its plumage, and when it comes out it will preen energetically. It won't preen unless it has been in water, but it must preen to repair all the damage to its plumage that the washing and handling will have caused, so regular access to fresh water is vital. There we hit a snag, in that our only tank was the bath. We would have to take our birds up to it, put them in and get them out again when they seemed to want it.

Over tea that Thursday, an inelegant snack taken standing among the remaining orange boxes, we pondered over the eleven dry birds on the floor, and the damp one by the Rayburn. We decided to let the dry ones have their first swim before we washed any of the others. We took them upstairs accordingly and very gently put them into four inches of water in the bath. For a minute or two they splashed around merrily and then, quite suddenly, they panicked. They were frantic to get out so we put them all on the bathroom floor where they settled down very quickly and then we took them downstairs again. Clearly, eleven were too many to have in the bath at one time, and we should have to stick to three or four in future. Clearly, too, the birds had brought most the water out of the bath with them, for quite soon it was coming through the kitchen ceiling.

Over the weekend we washed the rest of the birds and put them all in the bath for a swim, three or four at a time. We found we couldn't leave them alone for although most of them swam and dived impeccably the odd ones would try to get out and would have to be rescued. We had suffered some casualties but we still had eighteen birds, all eating well and apparently fit. The everlasting marching up and down stairs was a bit of a chore but we felt we were winning. True, none of the birds was entirely waterproof but we were pretty confident in our washing and rinsing, so the trouble must be due to feather disturbance and the birds themselves would soon sort that out.

But the birds weren't waterproof the next weekend, either, and we started worrying. There was no oil left on the birds – we could check that. It was hard to imagine that there was any detergent left on them, but that was impossible to check. We couldn't check the condition of the plumage, either, because to do so would require a microscope, would cause a lot of feather disturbance itself, and we weren't sure what to look for anyway. 'The birds will preen vigorously', we checked in the book, 'when introduced to clean water.' They certainly preened, but perhaps they were not preening enough, or vigorously enough. And if not, why not? Clearly, washing birds, like any other skill, was something where an hour's demonstration by an expert was worth a million words of instruction.

During the week, we realized that the birds' tails were beginning to get foul from their own droppings. The half hour or so they spent in the bath each day was evidently not enough for them to get themselves clean, but there was no way we could improve on it. Droppings, however, like any other contaminant, will wreck a bird's waterproofing, so we decided to wash a few birds a second time. We said we'd give them the full works; 'we'll get them clean this time,' I added, 'if it kills us'. In fact the job was much more likely to kill the birds!

We washed three birds, anyway, on a Saturday night, with extreme attention to detail, and afterwards decided to keep them separate from the others. We rigged up a makeshift partition in the kitchen, an old curtain draped over a couple of stools and the family play pen, as well as our old fire guard, and put the single-wash birds to the south, the double-wash birds to the north. On Sunday morning we put our three double-washed beauties in the bath and awaited developments with bated breath. Eureka! There was a definite improvement, so we washed all the others again.

Several days later little groups of birds were distributed all over the house, each group distinguished by a particular degree of waterproofness. There were some in our living room, some in the passageway leading to the kitchen, and two groups in the kitchen itself. Getting round the house was like an obstacle race. By now, too, the smell had become well seated. Between bits of food and the birds' droppings, the whole kitchen was pale grey to a height of about eighteen inches, and the smell intruded on all our activities, interfering with the enjoyment of everything from Brahms to bacon and eggs. Walls and doors were no obstruction. Yet we had to soldier on, because the birds had to be fully waterproof or they would surely drown as soon as they were released.

A week before Christmas, six of the birds were in a promising condition. As they now seemed to spend their daily half hour in the bath without the slightest sign of disaster we gave them a full hour, to make sure, and still they were dry. We asked Peter Davies of the Nature Conservancy, the bird recorder for Cardinganshire and the nearest licensed ringer to us, to come and ring them, and on the first fine calm day thereafter, we let go our six dry birds at the seashore. Off they went, diving and preening, and obviously at home in the deep waters. So far, so good and all the trouble and mess seemed less significant.

Five of the remaining dozen birds died during the next week, of aspergillosis, as the vet lab told us, and we learned that aspergillosis is generally only diagnosed post mortem. It is a mould which forms on the surface of the lungs and breathing tubes and kills before anything can be done. It results from the aspergillus fungus, the spores of which thrive on damp straw, which is why straw should never be used as bedding for seabirds. It is likely to be present, though dormant, in any bird, and will become active if the bird loses condition for any reason. So it is always liable to attack a wild bird in captivity, and we were assured that there was nothing we could have done that we had not done, except perhaps wash and rinse our birds more thoroughly the first time, to prevent it.

During the first week in January the surviving seven birds went back to sea, fit, fat and perfectly dry, and we had a grand scrub-up. The kitchen units returned to blue and white, the walls were repainted, and the partition went back into the loft. The smell took three days to go, but at last we had a house, not a fish-glue factory, to live in. We had a few minutes to sit down.

We were still in this euphoric condition when more oiled birds started turning up on the beaches, a mixture of razorbills and guillemots as before, and in much the same condition. Our sympathy for poor old Sisyphus increased. But we knew much better what to do now and the birds became waterproof much more quickly than before. We decided not to split the house up into pens, this time, but to devise some kind of identifying mark. Dymo tape seemed a good idea, but taken round the bird's leg and pressed sticky side to sticky side, it would not last long in water. A staple through the 'tail' prevented it coming apart but a natural reluctance to crimp the bird's leg in the stapler meant that some of the rings were too slack and came off. Webbed feet look very big when stretched, but they are surprisingly thin when the bird pulls its toes together, and a ring has to be a good fit if it is to stay on a bird when it is swimming.

We had twenty-four birds this time, and one of these was a guillemot we will not easily forget. The lad who found him called him Robert so we stuck to the name, too, even though his ring said Red Five. Most birds peck at their handler's hands when they are first picked up but Robert sat in the hand like a gentleman. When in the fullness of time, he was let loose in the kitchen, he tapped on the fridge door with his beak, squawking madly. A guillemot has a splendidly raucous call, but will usually stay quiet for at least a few days after capture. Robert found his voice four days before any of the others. In the bath, he obediently opened his wings and submitted quite cheerfully to all the other indignities of the treatment as if to the manner born. One evening, Robert was in the bath, washing himself merrily, when Jean suddenly said 'This bird's Pip. He's acting like Pip used to!' 'We can easily tell' I said, 'Pip had a little bit of web missing, on his left foot.'

We looked, and sure enough Robert had a little piece missing from the web of his left foot. We felt certain that Robert and Pip were one and the same bird, but of course we couldn't establish this finally. It would have been of enormous value if we had been able to, because a bird which had been cleaned and returned to the sea only to come in again because he had been oiled a second time would have proved that one can return a bird to the wild successfully even after four or five weeks in captivity. We always get Peter to ring our releases now, if it is at all possible, but at Pip's time this never occurred to us.

We made a terrible mistake with the first release of this bunch, one we have never repeated but which makes us go cold even after six years. As I've said, one has to make quite sure that a bird is well and truly waterproof before it is released, because while the quicker the bird is returned the better, if it is not waterproof it will not survive. We took our six, duly ringed, well fed, and, as we thought, dry, and released them in perfect conditions on a Sunday morning. They swam out, diving and preening as the others had alone, then suddenly, and almost simultaneously, they began to propel themselves on the water with their wings, each making for the nearest rock. Quite obviously they were not waterproof at all. Out where they were there was no way we could reach them. We waited for ages, but no bird moved so, in the end, we went home, absolutely shattered, believing that we had condemned six lovely little guillemots to death.

About five o'clock, the telephone rang, and a voice said 'My husband has just come in and says there are ringed guillemots all over the Quarry beach. One came right up to him and he's brought it home. Do you know anything about it?'

James Hunt couldn't have bettered my time to her house, and there in the kitchen, playing with the children and the dog, was Robert. With ecstatic thanks we put him in a box and charged for Quarry Beach. I went quickly to one end, Jean to the other, and when we met again I had a guillemot in each coat pocket, Jean had one under each arm, and the fifth one was at her feet waiting to be picked up. The day had been saved but only just, and we gave humble and hearty thanks for the saving of the birds and of our own consciences, and swore we would never make the same mistake again. (Unfortunately, many people do. In 1978 there was a news item on television about some birds cleaned of oil and ready for release, somewhere in Kent, but which were too tame to go. An RSPCA Inspector and some other people carried them into about two feet of sea, from which they flopped their way back ashore, showing all the signs of not being waterproof and knowing it. They were then taken five miles out to sea in a helicopter, where presumably they drowned.)

We made sure of ours, having had a second chance in the matter, and duly released them, with the other survivors, sixteen in all, a week later. The Newcastle recommendations had said that a recovery rate of better than half could be expected and we had achieved it − not by much, but we were the right side of the middle.

During the weeks that followed, we tried, subconsciously rather than deliberately, to balance our achievements with our troubles. Our achievement was little enough, twenty-seven birds out of forty-nine brought in, and who knew how many birds had also floated in dead or died at sea. Even so, twenty-seven was something, since guillemots and razorbills lay only one egg a year, and are particularly vulnerable to marine oiling.

More and more, our principal memory was of clean and fat birds returning to the sea and swimming happily away, and while nothing would expunge the memory of the mess and the smell and the obstacle course, and Jean trying to cook with twenty-three orange crates in the kitchen, each with a bird in it, its impact diminished with time. We realized, finally, that we were now established oiled bird cleaners and rehabilitators, and any oiled birds for miles around would come to us. We also realized that we could not imagine ourselves refusing to treat any sick or oiled bird which people brought us. Therefore, we must find a way of looking after such birds which left it possible to live in our own house while we were at it.

4
Getting Organized

Penfoel was little better than a ruin when we bought it, but we didn't have to pay very much for it, and we could do what we liked with it. By the time our thoughts turned to accommodation for birds, the old cartshed had become the dining room, and the old cottage contained our living room and the kitchen, with the bedrooms and bathroom upstairs. At the cottage end of the cowshed was the entrance hall and downstairs loo and cloakroom. The rest of the cowshed, measuring twenty-five feet by fifteen, still bore traces of its original use, in that the stepped floor was still there and it was easy to see where the stalls had been. We had quite enough house to live in without using the cowshed, and though both Honey and Sheba had a litter of puppies in it, it was not really being used except as a store room. Actually, storeroom is a euphemism. It was a junk hole. Deciding to set up a room to treat birds took a long time. Deciding where to put it was automatic.

Fifteen feet square would be big enough – the far-end fifteen feet at that, in view of the smell which would be generated. But curiously, I'm not sure why, though we have had far more birds in the bird room than we have ever had in the kitchen, smell has never in fact been a problem. When we have lots of birds in, the place is practically knee deep in fish, so a delicate aroma of Billingsgate is to be expected, but we never get the pong which used to pervade the kitchen when we kept birds there.

I duly concreted the cowshed floor to level it, put in a french window instead of an ordinary one, because we thought direct access to the great outdoors would be useful – and how right we were – fixed up a new ceiling, and plastered all the walls. For a fiver I bought a nearly-new steel sink complete with taps and waste, and I made a cupboard unit to match it, covering one wall. On the opposite wall I fitted shelves to hold the birds in boxes or cages pending washing, and pens to hold them after they had been washed. On the floor was a timber frame lined with a polythene sheet which made a splendid indoor tank, and on the wall by the window was a set of kitchen scales adapted to weigh birds (placed for the purpose in a bag). It all looked very professional, and we longed to have birds to treat in it. It was going to be so much more convenient than the kitchen, and we now ought to be able to save every bird brought in, not just better than half of them. We were also given some fluorescent lights for the room, which we gathered had been the property of the Ministry of Defence. I like to think the Minister was happy about the transaction.

Bill Hallam of the RSPCA was a regular caller during the construction phase and was always ready with advice. He was as thrilled with the room as we were. The local branch even decided to adopt the place and pay its expenses, and gave us a storage water heater and some cages. Offers of help came in from all over the area. I became vice-chairman of the RSPCA branch. We had, we felt, got it made. Now all we needed was some oiled birds, so that we could, at last, clean them effort-lessly, and get them back to sea.

The first patient to arrive at our new set-up was a guille-mot, but it died before we could wash it. Our second was a razorbill, which we cleaned and which was quite dry and only being fattened up a bit, ready for release, when it, too, keeled over and died from aspergillosis. It wasn't a very good start. Moreover, during the razorbill's stay, Jean was carted off to hospital for a considerable operation and took with her a magnificent bruise on her left shoulder where it had bitten her. A guillemot will jab at you with its pointed bill, but a razorbill, whose beak is much deeper and more rigid, will take firm hold of your skin and hang on. You can just about open his beak to get him off, or get someone else to do it, but if he is just pulled off he is liable to take a little piece of you with him. On the comparatively horny skin of the hands he won't leave much of a mark but on the soft skin of Jean's shoulder this razorbill had left a bruise about two inches across, varying from almost black in the middle, through various shades of purple, to pink on the edge. In the heat of the hospital the bruise was showing up high, wide and handsome.

'What did that?' asked the ward sister, the nurses, the porters, the anaesthetist and the surgeon, all in turn.

'You wouldn't believe me if I told you.'

'Try me.'

'A razorbill bit me.'

Only the surgeon believed her for somehow he knew about razorbills.

Almost every bird that comes in for treatment, whether oiled or injured, is to some extent dehydrated and immediate action is to feed it fluids. This can be done with a small spoon, but the easiest way is to use a hypodermic, without the needle, of course, though perhaps fitted with a piece of thin plastic tube, and gently squirt the liquid down its throat, giving the bird plenty of time to swallow. We therefore have a good deal of use for hypodermic syringes. Most of these nowadays come in sealed sterile packets and are only used once, but unless they have been used for something very nasty, which is unlikely, they are perfectly alright for giving birds a drink afterwards. When she was normal again, Jean realized that she was in the middle of a vast store of once-used syringes, and asked the

Night sister for some. Up came a box full, many of them new, with strict instructions to keep them out of sight and not to tell the Day sister. Next morning Jean tried her luck with the Day sister, who also came up with a full box.

'Don't tell the Night sister, whatever you do,' she said.

Shortly after Christmas 1973, and after Jean had come home from hospital, we were told that hundreds of common scoter, a kind of sea-going duck, had got covered in diesel fuel, leaked presumably from a fishing boat, and were coming ashore in huge numbers, all in their last stages. Thousands of them winter in huge rafts in Carmarthen bay, feeding on shellfish, particularly mussels, and they dive to tremendous depths to get them. Everyone interested in birds went to help, and very soon there were scoter in garages, bathrooms and spare bedrooms all the way from Tenby to Pendine.

We were asked to take some for treatment and on New Years Eve I went to Cardigan to meet a car which was bringing some birds from Tenby. I took charge of two large, heavy and suspiciously silent cardboard boxes. There were twelve scoter in one, fourteen in the other, and when I opened them up it was clear that a lot of birds in a big box is not a clever way of transporting them. There was ample room in each box, at least for the hour-and-a-half or so the birds would be in it, but they were not taking advantage of the fact and were all bunched up in a corner. The heat from the resulting pile was tremendous and three birds were already dead. Newcastle University had recommended that it was far better to transport birds over a long distance to a decently equipped unit for treatment than to attempt to treat them with no facilities. They should also have specified the use of small boxes, with only a few birds in each one.

I motored home with the boxes open, for the birds couldn't do much harm and at least I could clean up the mess. I anticipated a car full of loose and energetic ducks, but in the event, they stayed in their boxes, and I worried that they were too quiet by half. But they seemed none the worse for the rest of their journey and when I got home we split them up, fed them and dosed them. They took sprats very easily and all the assorted medicines as well.

All the guillemots and razorbills we had treated had been contaminated with crude oil, which showed up all too clearly on their white breasts; once the white feathers were clean, the chances of any oil remaining elsewhere were very remote indeed. Now we had birds that were completely black except for the yellow bills of the drakes, covered with a colourless contaminant, so there was no way we could see how well we had washed them. So we washed them as we had washed the auks, and rinsed them very thoroughly. Most of our previous birds had had two washes at least, so if we erred at all with the scoter, we overdid the washing and rinsing. We were mildly surprised, therefore, to find our birds were very far from waterproof. Not to worry, we said to each other, we'll let them rest for a day or two and then wash them again.

But the casualty rate was alarming. Apart from the three birds dead on arrival, seven more died the first night, and six more the following night. Admittedly the birds had been without treatment for days before we had them, but it was in our house that they died, and our hopes that we could save anything now we had a reasonably proper set-up were taking a beating.

When the second washing produced no improvement whatever in the waterproof qualities of the scoters' plumage, we rang Newcastle University for advice. We gathered that light fuel oils were particularly difficult to wash off, but we got no real advice as to what to do, as cleaning off diesel was something no one had then mastered.

We were having trouble with our free swimming set-up, too. We had to abandon the frame and polythene sheet, because the only way to empty it was with buckets, and sixty gallons is a lot of buckets. Then we tried an old bath, to which I fitted a nine-inch timber surround, with a ramp to get up to it, and treated the freeboard with glue and sand so that the birds could get a grip. The snag was that the rim of the bath was a foot or a little more above the floor of the pens, and the birds simply

refused to climb up to reach it. We had to get a tank whose rim
was not more than an inch or two above the floor level of the
pens, say a foot deep. Fortune smiled again, in that I found the
perfect tank, made of fibreglass on chipboard, six feet by three,
and a foot deep, built to demonstrate a pump at the Royal
Welsh Show and now sitting unwanted in its maker's yard. I
got it for a fiver. With some gentle chivvying, the birds passed
into this from their pens with no bother. They also came out
quite happily on their own, stood on a platform to drip, and
then returned one by one to their pens, where the food was.
We used to get them in three or four times a day, when they
would swim for ten or fifteen minutes until they started to get
wet, then come out. Soon they were well up to weight and the
best we could hope for was to keep them until they moulted
and grew new, clean feathers.

During February, we were told that thirteen birds were still
alive in South Pembrokeshire, none of them waterproof, and
would we please look after them, because no one else had the
facilities. We knew all too well what keeping birds was like
without a room to do it, so we said yes and in due course took
them over. One more had died in between times, and we now
had twenty-two birds. We settled into a routine, weighing the
birds every Saturday morning, identifying them by a coloured
ring so that records could be kept, and scrubbing the pens
thoroughly. If a bird had lost any weight we gave it antibiotics
and vitamin B12 to improve its appetite. Unfortunately, once a
bird started losing condition, it always died, whatever we gave
it.

It was during March that General Pugh, the chairman of the
County RSPCA branch which was now meeting our expenses,
decided that it was time we were properly Opened. The event
was to be a major occasion, and an obvious opportunity not
merely to publicize the work of the unit, which had by now
somehow acquired the name of New Quay Bird Hospital, but
also to raise funds. As his vice-chairman and nominal operator
of the hospital, he delegated the details to me, arranging for

Wynford Vaughan Thomas to come and make the actual opening.

We decided that the occasion should take the form of a coffee morning, so we wanted plenty of stalls to give all the people something to do and plenty of opportunity to spend their money, some at least of which would remain with us. Payment for admission would cover the coffee and biscuits. Things were likely to go on well beyond the normal coffee morning times, since Wynford couldn't come before noon, so we settled on a cheese and wine lunch, too. As we had no licence, we found we had to charge for everyone's chunk of french bread, his lump of cheese and his bits and pieces, and give him his glass of wine. To make it legal this had to be followed rigidly, so there was no way anyone could have his cheese without also his glass of wine. I wondered how many teetotallers would stay for lunch. We arranged for a raffle and, to involve the younger generation, a painting competition. The first Saturday in May was to be the great day.

It dawned bright and clear, which was just as well, since if it had rained we should have been ruined. The place looked great. There are half-a-dozen big cherry trees in the garden, as well as a couple of ornamental crab apples, and they were all in full blossom. About nine o'clock, we realized we had no change for cash floats for the stalls. So I had to rush madly around three shops, two garages and a pub, and when I got back the helpers were already arriving, and people were bringing in all manner of things to sell. The trickle of children's paintings became a torrent, and when displayed they covered both sides of seven eight-by-four sheets of whatever was available – plywood, chipboard, hardboard, plasterboard, which we were dead lucky to have handy. Thank goodness it was fine – there was no possible site for the paintings under cover. Apart from one or two anxious and highly competitive parents who would have preferred their offspring's contribution on a light background like ceiling board, for instance, rather than a dark one, like hardboard, we had no bother, except that as soon as we had all the pictures properly fixed up the judge rang up to say he wasn't coming. We had to arrange the judging for Monday.

By ten o'clock all the approaches were guarded, the cows had been persuaded to vacate the car park, the stalls were manned and we were ready for battle. At a guess, half the village was there helping, and we had a moment's worry that with so many people helping there would be none left to attend. We needn't have worried. People came in droves. The word had got around.

By 10.30 am the cake stall, which occupied the dining room, looked like the spring sales. By eleven o'clock it was cleared out and the faithful staff were getting the bread and cheese ready. Three dozen pairs of 'seconds' from Slimma Slacks had been very kindly donated, but the labels had been removed from them, so as there was no indication of size on the garments, they had to be tried on. When I went upstairs for something during the morning I found every room full of women in their knickers trying on trousers! Whatever it was I had gone up for went clean out of my mind.

Jean and I had decided that one of us should be in the bird room to explain what it was all about, while the other did the good-morning-how-are-you-good-of-you-to-come bit. The arrangement worked splendidly. The scoter, bless their hearts, went in and out of the tank several times more than usual and everyone thought it was marvellous. Eleven-thirty came, and we drew the raffle and auctioned a few of the more special items we had been given.

But at twelve o'clock there was no sign of Wynford. Should we start the cheese and wine before everybody started going? Fortunately he arrived just as I was opening the first bottle. I dashed outside to find that all those present had formed two lines, about six feet apart, and Wynford and I advanced towards each other between them, like generals meeting each other at a parade. I put on a smile of welcome, and must have looked like the original Cheshire cat by the time our hands met. Resisting the impulse to say 'Dr Livingstone I presume' I led him in. It was too late for the official opening ceremony so we all tucked straight into lunch.

By three o'clock most people had gone and by five the last person had drifted away, our friends as well. We were not too sorry, because by then we were exhausted, having bent the licensing laws a bit. Jean and I settled down to count the loot – there was a lot of it – and to restore the house to something like normal. We'd never had so much cash in the house in our lives. Counting it took rather a long time but restoring the house to normal took even longer.

The money went to the RSPCA, which was delighted with the take, and gave us in return a sixteen cubic foot second-hand freezer to keep food for the birds. Now we had a well-equipped unit to treat birds in, we had no financial worries, and on paper we were laughing.

One look at the obstinately waterlogged scoter, though, re-minded us that though we had a well-equipped unit to rehabili-tate oiled birds there was still a long way to go. We built a pen so that they could live outside, which we felt they might prefer, in fine weather, to being indoors, but for some reason they just huddled in a corner and looked far more miserable than they did inside. We brought them in again.

By September, it was clear that the birds' moult had gone all wrong, no doubt because they were in unnatural surround-ings, so the chances of them becoming waterproof that way were gone. It occurred to me to consult the Wildfowl Trust, since after all, scoter were ducks, and I duly phoned the Curator at Slimbridge, Mike Lubbock. He was very interested and asked a lot of questions, but, understandably, felt he couldn't help without seeing the birds. He asked if we would let him have them at Slimbridge, to see if he could get them clean there. It was a bit like asking a drowning man if he would like a life belt. I'm sure that if he had had his office windows open he would have heard me shout yes without the telephone. His wife, he said, and a colleague, would come down in a couple of days time to fetch the birds.

That night another bird died, and we prayed for the arrival of the Slimbridge duo while we still had some birds for them to take away. When they did arrive there were then only nine left, and these duly departed for Slimbridge, each one in an individual, upholstered compartment of the most beautiful travelling boxes I had seen. They never did get the scoter waterproof at Slimbridge, though, and they were still there eighteen months later when we drove over for a visit.

For the record, we now know how to clean birds which have been contaminated with diesel fuel. It took the very cold winter of 1979 to give us the information. My gritting lorries were getting stuck all over the place with 'frozen' diesel. Diesel fuel, I was told, contains a high proportion of waxes which crystallize at very low temperatures and form a gel, rather like hand cleanser, which the fuel pump will not pump. When a bird gets diesel on it, the volatile fractions evaporate, leaving the waxes on the feathers. The waxes are completely insoluble in water, whether there's detergent in it or not, hence the difficulty of getting a bird clean after contamination. The answer is to soak the bird in diesel again, or some other hydro-carbon solvent in which the waxes will dissolve, and wash the whole lot off before the light fractions have time to evaporate. It's easy when you know how.

The scoter departed for Slimbridge on a Thursday, and on the following Sunday we were asked to pick up an oiled guille-mot from the Harbour Master's office in New Quay. When we arrived the bird was standing on the back of a chair, just inside the open door of the office, not making any attempt to get away. He was desperately thin and the prognosis was bleak. All we could do was to feed him, dose him, dress him in one of our home-made ponchos, and put him in a box to rest. We were very surprised to find him alive on Monday, and more sur-prised still on Tuesday to find he'd put on an ounce in weight. By Wednesday night he'd put on another ounce so we washed him, and on Thursday, when we let him into the tank, he was completely waterproof. He put on two more ounces during the rest of the week so on the following Sunday, a week after taking him in, we put him back to sea and away he went as if he'd never left it. We called him Dickie, because the Harbour

Master's name was Richards, and we have much to thank him for. That one bird restored our faith in the Newcastle research team, our own unit, and ourselves. During the later stages of the sojourn of the scoter, we had a beauty of a problem, involving the RSPCA. In accordance with the RSPCA policy of moving its inspectors about every few years, Bill Hallam had, to much great regret, been posted to Church Stretton and we were beginning to find ourselves increasingly out of sympathy with the ways of his successor. By the autumn it had become plain to us that we could no longer remain on the branch committee and we therefore resigned. We were comforted by the knowledge that the Bird Hospital had collected and given more money to the Society than it, in turn, had spent on us, so we were pretty sure that we could maintain the unit by our own fund raising, but we did feel a bit lonely for a while. Had we really taken the only possible action under the circumstances or had we made a grand gesture which we were going to regret? Neither Jean nor I can fairly be described as resigners. We are both inclined to run up the battle flags and have a small war, if this seems to us the proper course. This certainly seemed a case for revolution, perhaps not for war, since continued association with this man would have destroyed our credibility as a treatment centre and rehabilitation unit, but if the revolution received too much publicity it would spoil the credibility of all the good Inspectors, like Bill Hallam. So, for good or bad, our consciences dictated that we resign.

Finance, of course, now became our big worry. It wasn't quite as easy to be self-supporting as we had imagined. We had raised more money for the RSPCA than it had spent on running expenses and on its contribution to fittings in the bird room, but we had also invested quite a lot of our money in goods for sale at Penfoel. For instance we sold ties, key fobs and badges bearing our logo – a guillemot preening itself, which a friend had designed for us – to supporters, and there were lots of other items as well. Making tow ropes was a particularly lucrative line. Our balance sheet would have looked fine but we had cash flow problems, since the cost of these goods had put the Bird Hospital account in the red, and I had to make this up out of my own pocket. I also discovered that quite large sums which had been collected by supporters in other towns and villages and given to the Society for our benefit had never been credited to the Bird Hospital account.

Then we had Moses, who ate altogether eighty stone, half a ton, of fish. He was easily the most expensive patient we have ever had. Moses nearly broke us, but it is fair to say that he was also the making of us. He was so very sick, and so very difficult to handle, that no patient is ever likely to be so big a problem again. Also, it was over Mo that we got to know Tom Herbert properly, and it was Mo who got us our Prince of Wales Award.

These awards are given annually either for architectural achievement or environment work, and each autumn I used to receive an invitation to submit for consideration any scheme I had carried out for the Council. Road schemes had to have something very special about them to qualify and though some of the Council's work in repairing and saving ancient stone bridges might have been appropriate I had no really good examples to propose in 1974. It seemed to me, though, that our own work with the birds might be on the right lines, so I took the papers home and we decided to submit our application. It would not need much preparation, it was worth a stamp, and if by some chance we got an award it would add a certain respectability to activities considered by many to be on the verge of lunacy. We filled the forms up, wrote up our history, enclosed some photographs, sent it off, and forgot all about it.

We were mildly surprised, then, to receive, by due appointment, an inspecting committee, which turned up in January to report on our activities. Two of its members knew us already, which was just as well. They did not stay long. It was the day of the England–Wales rugger match, when every true patriot without a ticket turns on his television, locks the door and puts the telephone off the hook. We forgot all about it again when they had gone.

We were, therefore, really surprised to receive in March a

second deputation, led this time by Lady Anglesey, who is vice-chairman of the Prince of Wales Committee, and including Brian Lymbery, its secretary. They arrived at 4.30 pm, and played with Mo for quite a time. At least he didn't actually bite any of them. Then we all had tea round the fire. By the time they left, over an hour later, they knew what books we read, what records we listened to, what we did, with the birds and otherwise, and what we intended to do. They were totally charming, and it had been a pleasure to meet them. They obviously realized what made us tick, and if we had received a letter to say our efforts were not quite what they wanted or were not quite up to their standard, we would have accepted it without question. If they had only been with us for five minutes and then turned us down, we would always have felt they had not properly found out what we were up to.

We then forgot all about it again, until Jean had a phone call from the *Guardian*, telling her we had an award and asking what we were really doing. Every other national paper, and most of the local ones, followed the *Guardian* during the day, and the following morning we received our official notification. I had rather too much gin at lunchtime.

We were duly summoned to attend a ceremony in Monmouth, in July, to accept the award. I was actually to receive it, and I could bring three people with me – Jean, obviously, Hugh, because he had had more to do with Mo than anyone, and Bill Hallam because without him we would probably never have started at all. I was to submit two slides, one of which was to be projected on a screen at the back of the stage, to show my particular project, when I went up to collect the Award. In due turn I went up to Prince Charles, against a background of a gannet fully twenty feet long, and received the award, the outward and visible sign of which is a considerable and very attractive plaque. Prince Charles asked me if I would have any trouble pinning it up. I assured him on that point.

The ceremony over, everyone adjourned to the Kings Head for tea. All the environmental awards bar ours, and almost all the architectural ones, too, had gone to councils, represented there by their chairmen. There was enough gold chain in sight to justify intervention by the Mafia. We four pushed off to a table well away in a corner, there to have some tea before disappearing home. I was one bite into a cucumber sandwich when I observed Lady Anglesey advancing towards us, with the Prince in tow. I had time to say 'on your feet' but not enough time to get up before they were on us.

'This is the bunch I wanted you to meet', said Lady Anglesey, as a preliminary. 'This is the bird hospital lot.'

The Prince and Lady Anglesey then joined us for about a quarter of an hour, though it seemed less at the time, during which we talked animatedly about seals. Prince Charles said he had just returned from Alaska, where he had been scuba-diving amongst them, and where he had had to accept and eat a plate of raw seal liver, something considered a great delicacy by the Eskimos who had offered it to him. He discoursed at length on its taste which, he said, was in keeping with the very distinctive smell of a seal, something with which, he understood, we were familiar. We were indeed, and sympathized exceedingly.

Compared with eating them raw, treating sick seals suddenly seemed a most pleasant operation.

5

The Birds and the Beaches

The joy of watching birds at their regular activities makes us feel that trying to help them when they need it is tremendously worthwhile. Obviously, our interest and pleasure in watching healthy wild birds is heightened by the details of their appearance which remains in our minds from the sick ones we have treated. Equally, treating a sick bird is made vastly more interesting by having watched the bird in the wild. We don't discriminate between species in our joy at watching them and we can't when they are sick – we will try our best for them all – but we have to admit to one or two favourites.

No one could fail to love a puffin. Puffins spend seven months of the year a hundred miles or more out to sea and only come ashore to breed. They do so hereabouts on the Pembrokeshire islands, Skomer and Skokholm, as well as on the bigger rocks of the coastal reefs. On the islands, each one lays its single egg in a burrow, a rabbit burrow if it can find one, and there are many available, but it will dig its own if it has to. Jean and I were having a picnic lunch on Skomer one day when we gradually became aware of one puffin which was circling us endlessly with a beakful of fish, while the others were coming ashore with a similar beakful each and darting down their burrows. When we moved along the grass, our puffin shot down a hole at the spot we had just left. Without realizing it, we had been sitting on his burrow.

The puffins not busy fishing or feeding their young stand about in groups, apparently chatting merrily to each other. The other auks, razorbills and guillemots, stand in groups, too, but solemnly study the seascape in front of them, like the members of a jury or a cartoonist's convention of clergy. Puffins, with their enormous, brightly-coloured bills couldn't look solemn if they tried, and in their groups they talk animatedly like wedding guests in the churchyard, while the photographs are being taken.

They are just as cheerful and friendly when sick as they are on their breeding grounds. Their lifestyle makes for very little contact with humans, so, as with the other auks, they don't have the fear of mankind that land birds have. It is always some time before razorbills or guillemots, loose in a room, will come away from the corners and watch what is going on, but a puffin will do so straightaway. It will sit on the worktop while you are treating another bird and watch you intently. While washing an oiled bird, one cleans its head with a toothbrush while the bird is in the washing bowl; a puffin will politely take the toothbrush from you and try to use it itself.

We've only actually had three puffins to treat. The first one died after a few days, in spite of all we could do, and subsequent analysis showed that it had died of a fantastic amount of cadmium poisoning in its body, but we failed to find out the source. The second turned up stormblown in Manchester and was looked after by Mrs Zalasicwicz of the Greenmount Bird Hospital, nearby. There are no puffin colonies nearer to Manchester than the Pembrokeshire ones and Mrs Zalasicwicz got so fond of him that, rather than take any chances at all with him, she brought him here so that we could organize his release among other puffins.

Our third puffin was oiled. Some visitors found him on Whitesands beach, near St Davids, so covered with the stuff that they thought he was just a lump of bitumen until one of them realized that the bright spot in the lump was an eye. When we got him waterproof we felt as if we'd won the war on our own.

Auks are the main sufferers from marine oiling, but puffins suffer most of all. Adult puffins weigh only half a pound and they spend their time at sea further offshore than the others. Being so small, they lack the reserves of strength to get to land when they get oil on them. Heaven knows we don't want puffins to be sick or oiled, but we enjoy treating any that are brought in. It can be a little distressing to realize that a bird for which I have nothing but affection and for which I am prepared to make every effort, doesn't trust me, but it doesn't happen with puffins.

The other seabird which never fails to excite us both is the gannet. It differs from the puffin in just about every way, being fifteen times heavier for a start, and while the puffin's wings beat like those of a bee to keep its little body aloft, a gannet's wings span six feet, all but an inch or two, and beat only fifty or sixty times a minute in level flight. Mother nature is a serious Goddess and usually designs her offspring for grace and elegance rather than for humour. Perhaps she made puffins just to show she really could make a lovable clown if she tried. She made up for it with the gannet.

A gannet lives on fish, which it catches by diving into the sea from a height of a hundred feet or more, closing its wings at the last moment. It catches its fish and swallows it before it surfaces. It is moving very fast when it hits the water, which it does with very little splash, but it is likely to be still moving fast when it takes its fish, and the impact then must be tremendous. The process of evolution has fitted it with an immensely powerful bill and neck, and therein lies the menace of a gannet at close quarters.

Gulls have formidable beaks and will bite you if they get a chance, but there's no harm in a gull. After it has chewed your finger for a while, and you have realized that it isn't hurting you enough to matter, it will look at you as much as to say 'This isn't getting me anywhere' and stop doing it. Then the problems of handling the gull are over. But a gannet has razor-sharp edges to its bill and if it chewed your finger in the same way it would cut the skin very badly indeed. If you are unlucky enough to get in the way when it takes a swing with its bill, the effect on your hand is like being slashed with a wood chisel. Worst of all, a gannet's neck is quite long and this makes your face vulnerable. The only safe way to get hold of a gannet, without gloves, is to throw a coat over it, get hold of its bill through the coat, then transfer your grip to the bird itself.

One day in 1974 Jean and I were down at Dale, in Pembrokeshire, where the falling tide reveals a huge area of mud in which there is a bed of razorfish, probably the best bait of all for bass, as well as every creepy-crawly described in a book. These attract a wonderful collection of wading birds and we watched them for ages. Other people were doing the same thing, and we fell into conversation with a couple from Hereford, Elaine and Ifor Evans. Naturally, in the fullness of time, we told them about our treatment unit at home.

The next day they found a baby gannet at Marloes, and they felt sure that there was something wrong with it. It couldn't fly, and it hadn't put up the sort of fight they had expected when they went to pick it up. We had taken a short break, in our caravan, at the time, and they brought the bird to us. An adult gannet is white, with black wing-tips, pale blue almost ice-cold eyes, and a glorious pale gold head and nape. A first year gannet is very dark browny-grey, with tiny white markings all over it. This was the first baby we had seen.

Parent gannets feed their solitary baby until it weighs about nine pounds, that is about a pound and a half more than an adult. They then desert it, and in time it leaves its nest, takes to the sea and swims about until, after a week or so, when its weight has come down, it takes off. We wondered, naturally, whether the only thing wrong with this bird was that it simply wasn't ready to fly. If that was the case, all we had to do was to take it a few miles out to sea and let it go. The temptation to do so was considerable, because it lived in a big carton in the lean-to of the van, and there was no way we could be sure that it and our labrador, Honey, wouldn't meet. It wasn't yet using its bill aggressively, but we were afraid it might start at any time, and a dog's face and eyes would be terribly vulnerable.

If it really was too fat to fly, the last thing it wanted was food, but if there was something wrong with it a little nourishment wouldn't come amiss. So Hugh and I caught some mackerel for it. It wasn't in the least interested, having so far only had partially digested fish, regurgitated for it by its parents, so we cut up a fish and gently force-fed it. We started calling it 'Gan', referring to it as 'he'.

We were due to go home five days after Gan came to us, and we became more and more concerned as to what to do with him. If the only thing wrong was that he wasn't ready to fly, it would be a nonsense to take him home with us. Equally, if there was something wrong, it would be a nonsense not to, but the only significant symptom he showed was inactivity, which we felt was wrong, but no one we were able to contact could tell us what his behaviour ought to be under the, admittedly unusual, conditions he was living in.

The problem was solved for us on the last morning. You can take a bird's temperature in the same way as for any other animal, but if it has a high temperature its bill will feel warm, in the same way as a person's forehead does, and this is easily detectable if the bird's bill is big enough. A gannet's bill is a fair handful, and while I was feeding him that morning I could feel that his bill was quite hot. So home he came, where we gave him a five-day course of antibiotics, during which his breathing became freer and his temperature came down. After another five days he developed an appetite and started showing an interest in his surroundings.

He still wouldn't take a fish from the floor, though, or from a dish or even in the tank. He wanted to be given it by hand, and since he was at a most impressionable age, this worried us. If in saving him from some kind of pneumonia, we had inadvertently taught him that food was obtained by humans opening his bill and popping it down his gullet, we had achieved very little. We sought advice and were assured that he would only regard us as an extension of his parents. We were told to release him at New Quay because this would be less of a shock to him than taking him near, or actually to, Grassholm, where he was born, and because when he was released he would make for West Africa where he would join hundreds of his kind and speedily learn all the lessons we had been unable to teach him. He would be able to navigate just as well from here as from Grassholm, we were blithely told, though just how he was going to do it no one was very sure. Much comforted, we fed him up to seven-and-three-quarter pounds, which seemed about right. Too heavy and he wouldn't take off, too light and he wouldn't have the reserves to carry him on his formidable journey. We had become very fond of this great bird that had sat so long and so impassively. We even bought him a ticket in a RAFA raffle, in Cardigan, and he won a box of sugared almonds. It was a good raffle for animals – a pet rabbit won a cookery book.

When Gan was up to weight, we took him down to the beach. I held him up for the pleasure of a last look at those enormous wings, he had a good flap in my hands, and I gently threw him forward into the sea. He splatted all over me. When returning birds to the sea, throw them gently by all means, but do it from your side as a threequarter passes a rugby ball, or you will be plastered all over. Off he went, in great style, and we went home rejoicing. We had treated, to our honest belief successfully, the biggest and allegedly the most ferocious sea-bird of the eastern Atlantic. 'Ha,' we said, Nothing to it!' How wrong can you be.

About a month later we had a phone call from Phyllis Bruce, the wife of the County architect in Aberaeron, asking us if we would take an injured gannet from her. Normally she would have loved to look after it herself – she was another of the breed whose husbands come home to find a notice on the front door saying 'Careful in the downstairs loo: Owl loose', but her granddaughter was being christened that day and she had a houseful of guests. She thought that the gannet needed attention urgently.

In the Bruce's drive sat a huge and very strong wooden box, with the gannet in it. There was no way we could get the box in the car so Hugh got out the carton we had brought and we went to get the gannet. The Bruces obviously had reservations about this. They offered gloves and other protective gear, all of which I politely declined – I thought I knew about gannets, and I was perfectly happy in what I was doing. Looking back it's clear that the Bruces knew what this gannet was like and that I had a higher opinion of my ability to handle him than was justified.

I opened the box and there it was, an adult bird with one wing hanging very badly. I held up one hand to attract its attention so that I could get hold of its neck with the other, happy in the knowledge that if I wasn't quick enough to get my first hand round the bird to hold its wings down, then Hugh would do it. The next instant, I was looking stupidly at my right hand, streaming blood, with a really deep cut right across all four fingers. I tried again, and this time my left hand got the same treatment. I was very tempted to postpone operations and go home for some real gloves.

Instead, I had another go, with a touch more attention to detail. This time I got hold of the bird's head while Hugh secured its wings. We transferred it to the carton, by which time it was covered in blood – mine, not the gannet's, though mixed with some of Hugh's. The carton would have been strong enough for dear old Gan one but it seemed a bit doubtful for this monster so we tied it up with a towrope, the only rope we had. It was three-quarters of an inch thick and I thought it was a bit of a nonsense on a cardboard carton, but the Bruces didn't think it was anything like strong enough.

The poor gannet's wing was not just injured, it was badly smashed. A bird's wing bones must be very stiff and strong as well as light, so they take the form of thin-walled tubes with stiffening gussets and diaphragms inside. These generally shatter on impact rather than break cleanly, so that an inch or two of bone will be in little bits. The only way to mend a break like that is to pin the fracture, using a pin of precisely the right length and diameter, then reassembling the bits and applying a cast to hold it all together. It's very much a vet's job, not an amateur's, and it's fortunate that broken bones in bird's wings are rare. The vast majority of 'hanging wings' result from strained muscles and tendons. To get a shatter type fracture to knit it is essential to have all the bits and for the break to be very fresh. In our case, the fracture was compound, an inch or more of bone was missing, and the break was at least a week old. There was no way our gannet could ever fly again, and euthanasia was recommended.

Euthanasia, whatever gloss you put on it, is a euphemism for 'kill'. We were being advised to kill the most magnificent bird we had ever seen, for its own benefit. It was the first time we had been faced with this decision and we found it a very difficult one to make. We were happy to play doctor or vet, but now we would have to play God, and we didn't like it a bit. Who could say that our gannet would be happier to be dead than to spend the rest of its life flightless, but much better fed and sheltered than it would be in the wild. Are animals happy in zoos? Any vet will attest to the fact that a distressing number of people who want their pet 'put out of its misery' only want to be spared the chore of nursing it. A flightless gannet, particularly one as ferocious as this one, would be a formidable and very expensive liability, but to be fair to ourselves, we didn't let that influence our thinking. We decided, finally, that our bird's ferocity showed that he felt a need to defend himself against us, so his life with us would be one of constant tension and not likely to be much fun, so poor Gan Two succumbed to an overdose of phenobarb. In a way, it was like Moses. Nothing would ever be quite so bad again.

As I said earlier, a sick bird is made vastly more interesting by having watched that bird in the wild. When we are treating a sick or oiled gannet, for instance, we think of it majestically airborne and picture it taking its fish. Regular sallies to watch healthy birds give one determination to treat sick ones and so we visit our local beaches a lot. A love of the sea plays its part in this, of course, with the seabirds as a bonus.

Except when it is known that there are oiled birds coming in and beaches are being regularly patrolled to pick them up, no one sets out specifically to find sick birds. People just go bird-watching and find the sick ones by accident. Their reactions on finding one vary. Fortunately, more people then ever before, will go to endless trouble to look after it or travel long distances to find someone they think will be able to care for it better than they can; others, sadly, will either ignore it or throw things at it. But appearances can be deceptive. One day two fellows turned up at Penfoel, cartoon Hells' Angels in appearance, studded leathers, knee boots, huge motor bikes, the lot. One of them was covered in blood. It turned out to be from a herring gull they had rescued from people who were stoning it!

Many people think that a sea bird should be either floating or flying, and if they find one on the beach they will either chase it into the sea or, if they can catch it, throw it up in the air, all with the very best motives. Poor bird. If it could float or fly it wouldn't have come ashore, certainly not on a beach with people on it. Immediate action with a dolphin or porpoise which has beached itself is to carry it into water deep enough for it to swim, but not with any other mammal and certainly not with any bird.

First catch your bird must be the watchword of anyone wishing to bring a sick or oiled bird in for treatment. A bird which lets you pick it up is pretty far gone; the harder a bird is to catch the better chance it has of surviving, but any bird which cannot fly will be in a state of shock and too much chasing will weaken it badly or even kill it on the beach. A trout landing net is an ideal tool for the job, but the first priority is to crowd the bird towards the back of the beach. A seabird's instinct is to get to the water and once he has made his mind up he'll go like lightning. Four times out of five a guillemot will scoot between the legs of a group of people trying to surround him, unless they know what to expect. If you can't catch your bird in daylight, wait until dark. He won't move far then.

The best oiled-bird catcher for miles around here was Evan Roberts of Llanrhystud, because he had a big black labrador which did it for him. The dog would catch the grounded birds with far less fuss than humans would, and when he had cleared the beach he would swim out and collect them in the sea. This was really something, because guillemots and razorbills, the birds he was catching, dive when approached in the water, and it is generally accepted that oiled birds cannot be caught until they beach themselves. Nets from helicopters are no use, and two scuba divers we know who spent nearly an hour catching an oiled razorbill were totally exhausted by the time they had managed it. Unfortunately, so was the bird, which died half an hour after being captured. Evan's dog could catch them, though, goodness knows how.

The Royal Society for the Protection of Birds organizes regular beach patrols to obtain information about normal sea-bird mortality. This is called the Beached Bird Survey, and volunteers visit every beach in the country during the last weekend of the autumn, winter and spring months to report the number of dead birds they find, particularly those with oil on them. These volunteers, working under an organization set up by the West Wales Naturalist's Trust, consitute the backbone of our local oiled bird collection set-up. In an oiling emergency, the Trust office is constantly manned, beachhead centres are set up with ample supplies of things like cartons and ponchos and a taxi service brings the birds from the beaches first to collection centres then to treatment units. These splendid arrangements are relatively new. Before they existed Jean and I can remember all too well being beseiged with phone calls from worthy citizens, ringing from as much as sixty miles away, with the dread message 'We've found an oiled guillemot on so-and-so beach. What should we do with it?'

Walking beaches for the pleasure of it, and to watch all the birds, is something we all should do more often. There is no end to the things one will see. I have already said much about the joys of watching gannets, but there are many more birds than gannets. A cormorant with a good sized flatfish is well worth watching, and so is a cormorant with a big eel. The bird will surface with the flat fish, held securely in his bill but wriggling furiously. He will beat it on a rock, turn it round, and beat it some more. He will beat its head, its tail, and both sides, which suggests to the watcher that the cormorant either has little experience of flatfish or is a trifle thick, because the fish will not have been in the least affected by his exertions and will still be struggling violently. He will ultimately try to swallow his fish, and will try, without success, to fold it up. Finally, and the battle up to that point may well have lasted half an hour, he will get it part of the way down his neck still wriggling visibly. At this stage he will consider that his fish is safe, so he will make for the horizon, looking like a Guinness advertisement.

Perhaps cormorants don't often get hold of big eels, either, or maybe eels are a serious problem to a cormorant, however many he catches. The cormorant tries to keep his eel untwined, so that he can wave it about like a whip and beat it on any handy rock, but given the slightest chance the eel will wrap itself round the bird's head until his bill is held fast against the neck. The eel will unwrap itself eventually and the bird will carry on whipping, but the eel soon finds something else to hold onto – a rock, or the bird's foot, and tries to pull the bird's head under water to drown it. The cormorant usually wins but the battle lasts for a long time.

Once we happened to be on our nearest beach, Cei Bach, which is Little Quay in English, when the Cardigan Bay flock of fulmars came in from the sea. Herring gulls are no mean performers in the air, but for sheer grace and apparent effortlessness they are clumsy amateurs compared with fulmars. A fulmar will stay aloft indefinitely without a wing beat, it will swoop from sea level to a point a hundred feet up the cliff, and pass a potential nest site or its actual nesting site, at every circuit, just as if it was going to land but changed its mind at the last moment. It will do this for an hour or more, its only wing motion being to steer or brake – perpetual motion personified. The scientific part of the watcher's mind will tell him the bird is using up-currents of air resulting from the breeze striking the cliff face, but the romantic part of his mind will tell him just to enjoy it while he has the chance.

A pair of fulmars are not unusual on Cei Bach. On this particular night there were hundreds. We started to count them, as they came in, but soon gave up as the spectacle grew. It would have been like counting the Tiller girls or the repeats in the last movement of Brahms's fourth. They arrived, flying straight and level, but as soon as they reached the cliffs they broke off into the most amazing display of aerobatics that I've ever seen. There was no pattern to it, and yet it seemed coordinated. The sky was full of fulmars, swooping at very high speed, but there was never even a near miss, let alone a collision. It is a sight which, I have read, Hebrideans and Orcadians see regularly, but it is very rare at Cei Bach. It lasted for the better part of an hour, after which all the birds, bar two pairs, dispersed.

There is really no limit to the variety of creatures which can be seen by the diligent watcher. About two miles this side of Cardigan is a lovely little beach called Mwnt, backed by cliffs whereon are green fields and a tiny, isolated church. One beautiful evening in September mine was the only car in the park and I was looking over the beach, straight into the setting sun. In quite shallow water was a head. It could only be a seal. I had read that if you whistle to a seal, it will come to you, so down I went to test the theory. The head came up periodically each time closer in, and I whistled the more furiously. You must realize that I was looking straight into the setting sun, all this time, and the sun was by now just touching the water. The head showed in about two feet of water and I was just wondering what I was going to do with the seal when it came out of the water, when it suddenly stood up.

Seal? It was a very shapely girl of twenty summers or thereabouts, dressed in a mask and flippers, and nothing more. This is quite a common sight in some places, I understand, but not very usual round here. I said good evening as she passed, pulling off her flippers, and she responded. I studied the sunset for what felt like a week, and, having decided that my seal must have got herself dressed by then, turned to find her alongside me in a sweater and slacks. She explained that swimming in the nude was her great joy, that she could only do it in the autumn when there was no one about and she apologized in case she upset me. She feared that someone would sooner or later complain and she would have to stop. I reassured her on this, and explained about the seal idea, but I don't think she was really listening. I'm sure I didn't convince her that a human head with a diving mask really does look like a seal's head in silhouette!

6

Aristocrats in Trouble

To maintain a reasonable bird treatment operation some degree of acceptance by local people is essential. Without it they won't bring in sick birds, or help you when you need help, and they won't contribute to your funds. Curiously, the more that people think you're crazy, the more you'll be in business. I served with the Chindits during the war, and most of the activities of that force would have led to its members being certified in peace time. My CO was Brig. J. M. Calvert, DSO, known universally as Mad Mike, and so far from the title being derogatory it was the biggest accolade his men could give him. It has never bothered me, either, to be described as round the twist – far from it. I was once introduced to a man who makes his living by operating hot air balloons with the words, 'You must meet this chap. He's as mad as you are.' I loved it. The man to watch, however, is the one who introduces you with, 'This is Mr Bryant. He, er, runs a, er, bird hospital near New Quay.'

The Prince of Wales award helped enormously in showing that someone other than ourselves attached value to our efforts. On one side of our front door sits our symbol, superbly done in wrought iron, a foot square, while on the other side is the award plaque. It has lent a great respectability to our particular brand of lunacy. It has also meant that we've had a lot more publicity for our work, and that in turn has led to all sorts of beautiful birds being offered or brought to us.

In May of 1975 Jean had a phone call from a frantic newsagent in Lampeter, who said that there was a baby owl in his storeroom which had terrified his cats, and would we please get it out because no one would go in. Jean couldn't contact me as I was out of the office, so she rang Bill Stratford in Lampeter. Bill had been the local manager of the Gas Board while gas was being made in Lampeter, during which time he and I had become sworn enemies because he used to dig my roads up with the enthusiasm of an overactive mole. When the town went over to the North Sea product he left the Board, and took over its showroom. In the front, his wife, Dot, purveyed boots and shoes, and in the back Bill bred exotic and very beautiful Australian birds. Would he fetch the owl, Jean asked? Bill was never one to refuse such a challenge and soon he arrived at Penfoel with a baby tawny owl which we called William, after its rescuer.

William stood about six inches tall, an almost spherical bundle of down, and we installed him in a tea chest with a wire front. After a day or two of persuasion he began to take plain meat quite readily off a pair of forceps, and after another day or two we wrapped up his meat in dog hair or chopped chicken feathers. In due course, as a result, he threw a pellet, which was placed on a dish and proudly shown to me when I got home. His digestion was alright, anyway. In no time, he was perching happily, watching what was going on outside the tea chest, his head rotating in the way that only owls can. If he was approached he would make astonishingly loud clicks, apparently with his beak. When he swallowed, his face moved exactly as I would think a very cruel cartoonist would depict a toothless geriatric. Soon he started eating on his own, and we sent out an SOS for mice. The neighbours responded nobly, and people motored amazing distances to bring us mice rescued from their cats. We would come home, too, to find anonymous packets of well-wrapped mice pushed through the letter-box. William thrived on this rodent fare, so we put him in a big pen in the garden, to get him accustomed to the look of the great outdoors.

By the end of July he was fully feathered, flying round his pen perfectly, and was ready for release, save for one thing. In the wild his parents would have taught him that his function in life was to catch mice and voles for food, and would have shown him how to do it. With the best will in the world, we could not help him there. Furthermore, owls are mildly terri-tory-conscious, and a newcomer is more likely to be chased away than accepted. Unless he was in the company of other owls which he could watch and emulate, we feared he might not get the idea of life in the wild, and if he was driven away he would not come back to us for a meal.

This problem solved itself during August and September. In August William found his voice, and in no time at all, tawny owls from miles around were coming to call. They perched on the tree branches all round his pen, and serenaded him and each other for hours together. By mid-September dozens of owls were arriving at Penfoel every night, so one evening, by which time we felt he must have properly met all his neigh-bours, we crept out and opened his pen. In the morning he had gone, but one particular owl stayed on nearby for many months afterwards, taking up a place on a low branch in the garden, even though we would shine a torch on him at night, and allowing us to get almost within touching distance before flying off.

Owls are mostly nocturnal so all that most people see of them is a flash in the headlights. Some people think their hooting is an eerie sound. Jean has a favourite aunt who would stay with us much more often if there were no owls about. Certainly our neighbours in Cardiff didn't like them. Being more used to them, perhaps, Jean and I love them. They can hoot all night without disturbing us, and we often go out on a moonlit night, when we can hear owls near us, in the hope of seeing them.

We can't keep crippled birds, just to keep them alive, but we once made an exception in the case of an owl. Someone had shot a pair of shorteared owls, crippling both of them. One of them died more or less immediately, the other was brought to Penfoel with a smashed wing. Tom Herbert did all he could, but gangrene set in and half of one wing had to come off. There are very few shorteared owls about, and this one had endeared himself completely to us by the time we had to come to a firm decision about his future. We looked at his huge yellow eyes, at the little tufts of feather which look like ears, and at the way he sat trustingly, on a perch or on my hand. By the time we knew he would never fly again we had become too fond of him to kill him. We felt we would sooner or later be able to find another flightless shorteared, but, alas, poor Sailor, which is what we called him, is still waiting for a mate.

We had a happier session in the summer of 1979 with an even rarer specimen, a little owl. A lady in Llannon, which is about ten miles from here, burnt some rubbish in her living-room grate after having no fire for some time. Little owls had nested in her chimney, and several shot out upwards into the air but one, along with a great deal of soot, came down into the room. The eyes of a little owl have a yellow ring round them like the shorteared, brighter, almost fluorescent, and as the bird was also totally black with soot, it nearly frightened the life out of the lady. The owl was equally scared, of course, and shot all over the room, while the poor woman thought she had some kind of hobgoblin in the place. Fortunately it wasn't long before she realized what she was dealing with, that she needed the vet not the vicar, so she scooped the owl up and took it to Tom Herbert, and thus we came by Sooty.

There wasn't much wrong with him actually. He was a bit singed in places, but nothing very serious, and he was covered in soot, which he managed to get off himself although it took a week before he had reached his proper colour. He'd lost the tip of his upper mandible, too, but not enough to stop him feeding.

Releasing him was a bit of a problem because we wanted him to join others of his kind but no one knew where to find them in Llannon. Fortunately there is a colony of them living in an old lime kiln on the island of Skomer and that's where he went.

Snowy owls no longer breed in this country but the Hawk Trust is trying to re-establish them by breeding them in captivity and releasing fledged babies in places where they might nest. A falconer friend of ours, Carl Jones, was bringing up a pair of babies and called here for us to see them. A snowy owl stands roughly twice as tall as a tawny, so although they were just about spherical like William had been, they were twice as big. They wandered all over the living room on their enormous talons, looking like gigantic grey-and-white powder puffs. The dominant memory I have is of their eyes. Birds require very acute vision, so they have eyes larger in proportion to their size than mammals, and owls have bigger eyes than most birds, being nocturnal. But the eyes of these two snowy fledglings really were enormous, and deep and unfathomable as well. To be stared at by a snowy owl, even a baby one, is quite an experience.

Of the regular indigenous owls, the barn owl is probably the most dramatic. Its numbers are dropping fast because it likes to live in unoccupied buildings and there are not many about. Round here, old buildings are either done up as summer cottages or demolished to make room for modern buildings. The back and head of a barn owl is a wonderful mini-paisley pattern in muted shades of blue-grey and brown. One of the big thrills we have had from treating sick birds is the opportunity it has given us to drool over the plumage of barn owls. But its breast and underparts, and the under-surface of its wings, are brilliant white, and this is the only aspect of the bird most of us see. Its call is a real shriek, all right for someone who knows what it is but distinctly unnerving to strangers.

Three of us went sewin fishing one night – sewin is the local name for sea trout – and took a visitor from the Midlands with us. We parked our bags under a big oak tree near the river. After some time I went back for something and as I got near the tree a barn owl flew into the branches. The Midlander was there before me, fiddling in his bag, when the owl hooted. 'What was that' he gasped out in the kind of voice usually reserved for television actors in shows like Dr Who when a twenty-foot spider looks in at the window. I was just about to tell him, when the owl flew off, white and silent, a wraith in the moonlight. That did it.

I saw a man in the same sort of panic once before, a clerkly type, unused to explosives, who came with me on a visit to a quarry. When he found that the word printed on the box he was sitting on was Gelignite, not Glengettie, he took off and didn't stop for a quarter of a mile. My fishing friend would, I think, have given much to emulate him that night, but his legs wouldn't move, and though his mouth was open he was speechless. He remained rigid, staring at the point in space where he'd last seen the owl. I tried to explain, but I might as well have been talking to the tree, and I was getting really worried when the other chaps came up and between us we got him out of his paralysis and sat him down. But he was shaking far too much to pack up his own tackle so we had to do it for him, and then we took him home. He uttered not a word on the way.

I well remember our first barn owl, Jonathan, who was brought in from Crymych with an injured wing. His left wing hung a good inch below the other, so we strapped him up to take the weight off his injured muscles and let him rest. After three weeks, during which he fed himself like a gentleman and threw pellets regularly to show he was happy with his diet, we took the strapping off and to our delight he was symmetrical again. Even so, we were worried as to just how fully his muscles had healed. A bird released after wing damage is in much the same position as a man who has to make a living by manual work the day he is released from hospital.

We discussed this with a falconer friend who gave us a pair of jesses which we duly fitted and attached to a long, light line. We took Jonathan out into our flattest field, put him on the ground while I held the line, giving him about twenty feet of slack. In due course, off he went in the air, with me in tow, and just as I was getting near the hedge I lowered my end of the line to the ground and found that Jonathan came down, too, just like a kite. We only gave him a few minutes the first time, extending his practice periods over the next fortnight, by which time we were satisfied his wing was fully restored. I recommend the process to anyone with a weight problem. It is surprising how fast an owl flies.

We made a box, to RSPB specifications, set it up in our barn, and put Jonathan in it, with food and water, but with a little wire door which we kept closed at first. After a few days we opened the door, by which time he had established his own smell and general presence on the box. I suppose it was too much to hope he would live in it thereafter, for he disappeared a day or two later, after which he set up home in Sefton Farrel's barn across the valley. All the other barn owls we have had have always left us soon after their repairs. I wish a pair would settle in our own barn, for it is just the right sort of home for owls to nest in and there's enough live stock in it for an army of owls. One day perhaps.

The predatory birds, the raptors, are the aristocrats of the bird world, and it is always a thrill as well as a challenge to treat a sick one. Hawks and falcons are like racing cars, sleek, fast, highly tuned and not for the inexperienced. The briefest association with a raptor is enough to show why falconers are willing to spend weeks with a single bird, training it and getting it used to human presence. Surprisingly, for such up-market birds, they have a strongly developed head-in-the-sand syndrome. If they can see no danger they will be quiet and happy. Even the best-trained falcons are normally hooded when they are being carried about. The wildest bird will be quiet and content in a closed box or in the dark or hooded, but it will suffer terribly if it is kept in an open cage with people about. Raptors can literally be frightened to death. Every time a captive one is disturbed, even a little bit, it secretes enormous amounts of adrenalin and in a few days this can so upset its whole system as to cause death by kidney failure.

Sparrow hawks move like greased lightning. Our first one, from her size a female, came in unconscious, with a chaffinch – also unconscious – which she had been chasing when they both flew into a plate glass window. The chaffinch recovered very quickly and we released him in the garden, but the hawk was quite groggy for a while. She suddenly woke up on the second evening and got loose in the treatment room. There was no way of getting near her. She shot like a bullet between anything in the room she could perch on, and it was obviously hopeless to catch her without real risk of damaging her. From the way she was behaving, though, there was probably nothing to worry about, so we decided we would just open the windows in the morning and let her go.

Later in the evening, I went into the treatment room for a last look around, and to turn off an infra red lamp which was helping to dry off a guillemot. In the subdued light the hawk sat perfectly still, and to my great surprise she allowed me to pick her up, with no apparent alarm and certainly no resistance. There was clearly nothing wrong with her to prevent her release the following morning. She was a particularly fine specimen of a sparrow hawk and remained in and around Penfoel for several weeks, taking one of our doves every morning.

Kestrels are very beautiful, too, but very vulnerable. They are so nearly motionless when they hover as to be prime targets for air guns, and the film *Kes* has made all too many people want one as a pet. We were unwise enough once to start playing with an orphaned baby one, something we are normally very careful to avoid, and in no time it was perching quite happily on Jean's or my shoulder and before we realized what was happening it had become imprinted on us. An imprinted bird cannot be released to the wild because it will rely on humans to feed it, and when it flies away from 'home', as it will sooner or later, it will attack people when they don't feed it.

One way or easing an imprinted bird back into the wild is to tether it by the usual falconer's leash, about two feet long, to a ring running on a fixed line about ten feet long in some cat-proof location like a flat roof. At one end of the line should be a box to give the bird shelter, and at the other the bird's food. The bird will get used to the spot where its food is put and so will keep coming back to the same place after its release. In time, it will come less and less regularly as it begins to find all its own food in the wild.

We were not able to do this with our kestrel because we have a herring gull called Spotty who came to us as a tiny chick, years ago, and has never left us for longer than the odd day since. No kestrel tethered on a roof would have much chance of feeding with Spotty about, so we had to get a falconer friend to look after our baby and finally to release him.

Any bird of prey, incidentally, should be handled with gloves on, irrespective of size. Its bill won't do much harm but its talons can. They are exceedingly sharp and can easily penetrate human skin, so there is a real danger of deep-seated infection if they are dirty. You are quite safe holding a bird with both hands round its body and wings and its legs between your fingers, but its natural instinct is to perch and when you relax a little, as you surely will, it will grip your finger. That is when you'll wish you had gloves on, because the power of a raptor's talons is incredible. It will normally exert only enough pressure to enable it to remain stable on your hand, but occasionally, perhaps as a human being will put all he's got into a good stretch, a bird will really use its strength. I once had a buzzard perching on my finger, with its talons right round it. I was just reflecting how regal the bird looked when it started tightening with one foot and just kept on tightening. It was like being caught fast in a set of pipe grips, and although I was wearing hedging gloves that buzzard really hurt. If he'd used the same power to grip the edge of my hand, his talons would have gone clean through.

Buzzards are quite common hereabouts, and we nearly always have at least one as a patient. Diagnosis is a real problem. There is a real danger that a thorough examination will trigger the sequence of events which ends with kidney failure after five days. So unless there is any obvious injury we give a buzzard glucose solution, vitamins, antibiotics and a little raw meat, then pop it into a closed box where it can rest in peace, and, we hope, eat the meat we will have put in for it. The temptation to have a peep now and again, to see how the patient is doing, is tremendous, but we have learned to resist it. One disturbance, or at the most two, daily, for feeding and other attention, is the limit, and if the bird is still alive after a week, there is a good chance of saving it.

Once a buzzard has passed this apparently critical period, it seems to recognize that you are trying to help it, and will co-operate all it can. Biggles was a buzzard we had from the plant-breeding station just north of Aberystwyth, a very pale one, almost grey, with a huge lump over his left eye. It gave him a curiously raffish appearance, not at all unattractive, but as he was not much more than a skeleton the lump was likely to be something unusual. One side of the lump seemed weaker than the rest, so every time Jean fed him she put Savlon on it. After a week, the skin opened and a thing like a hazel nut, in appearance as well as size, popped out and landed on the floor. The vet lab in Aberystwyth assured us that it was no more than dry skin, and that it was not malignant, but they could give us no explanation of its cause. The crater it left closed up in a day or two, leaving no sign, but poor Biggles also had another lump, the size of a big plum, on the 'false knee' joint of his left leg. The 'false knee' is the joint of a bird's leg which looks as if it ought to be the knee but bends the wrong way. The true knee is usually concealed in the feathers.

Hard bits of black stuff showed through the skin of this lump, so Jean treated it liberally with Savlon to soften it and regularly extracted the black bits with forceps. Biggles used to lie on his back while this was going on, unrestrained, which meant that Jean had to reach over him to get at the infected joint. She worked on this with a binocular magnifier on a head band which brought her face within easy range of Biggles' unrestrained and uninjured right foot. Never once did he strike out with that foot or even hint that he might, but sometimes he would clench it a little, and Jean always took this as indicating he was being hurt and stopped what she was doing. She got heaps of black stuff out of the lump and sometimes a little pus as well, but never found anything that might be taken as the seat of the trouble, and sadly the black stuff reformed almost as soon as it was cleared. Tom Herbert confessed to being baffled, and was afraid to operate for fear of cutting some of the blood vessels, nerves and sinews which must have been somewhere in the lump. Damage to any of these would, sooner or later, have finished poor Biggles, because a buzzard, unlike, say, a gull cannot live on one foot.

Jean worked on that leg for six weeks. Sometimes the lump would get smaller, and we crossed our fingers that her treatment and the regular antibiotics Biggles was getting were jointly doing the trick. But then the lump would get bigger again, and we would be back to square one. Tom was wonderful, and gave him every suitable antibiotic he could think of, but Biggles died in the end.

It was Biggles' acceptance of his treatment which so impressed everyone and so endeared him to us. Every night Jean would pick him up, carry him over to the table, under the light, and prod away at his lump. He must have known what was coming every time she went to fetch him. We feel sure that he knew we were trying to help him, and he played his own part superbly. We failed to save Biggles, but many people more knowledgeable than we, namely other vets from the area who visited him, had also been unable to determine what was wrong with him, so we don't blame ourselves unduly. In fact, that experience has since given us a greater confidence that other birds, particularly other buzzards, actually realize that we are trying to help them, even if we hurt them accidentally, and that in some way, after the first shock of capture has worn off, they trust us.

The legs and feet of raptors are scaly, and casual observation would suggest that they are tough enough to withstand practically anything. In fact, they are quite delicate, and prolonged use of an unsuitable perch, too fat, say, or too thin or with sharp corners, or no proper perch at all, will first set up corns, then bacterial infection with inflammation and finally abcesses. Prolonged perching on one foot will have the same result. This was brought home to us with horrible clarity in 1978.

On Easter Sunday, Mrs Myfanwy Evans, of Aberporth, who has been a tower of strength to us, both in bringing in sick birds and in raising funds, was having a picnic with her daughter and son-in-law when they became aware of a strange flapping noise nearby. They investigated and found four pole traps. These are spring traps fastened to posts, fence posts for instance, so that when a bird lands on one it is trapped by the leg. This is usually broken so the bird hangs head-down until it dies. Gamekeepers used to use them to kill predators which might take their pheasant chicks, and although they have been illegal for years the odd farmer still uses them to catch crows, which attack young lambs. One of these traps had a dead buzzard in it, one a dead crow, the third a little raptor so long dead as to be unidentifiable and the fourth held a live buzzard with one foot nearly severed.

Our friends brought the live bird to us and we took it to Tom Herbert on the spot. He showed us that although the leg bone might mend there was no way he could rejoin the severed blood vessels and gangrene would be inevitable, so the foot had to come off. Four days later, by coincidence, we had another buzzard with exactly the same injuries, from a place fifteen miles away.

Both birds healed well, and our contacts in the world of hawks and falcons thought there was a good chance of them returning to the wild successfully. One of these, Laurence James, with more knowledge of raptor treatment and behaviour than we had, offered to take them over and ease them back to the wild, and we willingly accepted. All went well for a while but after a time both birds developed trouble in the remaining foot and both had to be put down.

We never could find who trapped the second bird but the police and the RSPCA went to see the farmer who was responsible for the first one. They told us that, much as they would have liked to, they couldn't make a case against him so he got away with as callous an act as I have ever encountered. The indifference to suffering shown by anyone who sets a pole trap is quite incomprehensible to me. He is condemning to as hideous a death as the imagination can devise any bird unlucky enough to cross his traps, probably with no gain to himself. Buzzards don't hurt farmers.

Fortunately for our morale, one of our happiest stories was starting at just the same time. It concerned two buzzards again. Glyn came in first, a dark bird, very weak and thin. What actually ailed him we never knew, but he responded to peace, quiet, vitamins, antibiotics and food, and in due time we released him. As soon as he had gone, in came Sandy, a much paler bird and much bigger, suggesting that they were a pair, with one white primary feather in her left wing, and a broken leg. The primaries are the big wing-tip feathers, the main flight feathers, and her white one made her probably unique and certainly easily identified. Unusually in broken bird-bones, her fracture was not compound and was quite fresh. The best chance for the leg was obviously to have it set at once so, trying to balance this against the greater danger from shock and stress, off we went to Tom Herbert again.

Applying a plaster bandage is almost certain to be effective provided the two ends of the broken bone can be held properly mated, and this was not difficult to do in Sandy's case because the break was midway between the 'false knee' and the foot. Sandy settled down very quickly and was feeding herself in a week. She was flexing the talons on the splinted leg and in two weeks was putting weight on it. After three weeks we took the plaster off. By then the plaster will be as hard as rock and the little bone it encircles not much stronger than a match stick. It seems so easy to break the bird's leg again while getting the plaster off. Jean usually holds the bird while I first soak, then cut, then soak and so on, using a very sharp knife with an almost square end to the blade and a pair of scissors ground to almost nothing. In Sandy's case the job was enlivened by her large and very active talons between my hands. It was like wiring up a junction box with the power on, but the challenge simply added to the pleasure of seeing the firm sound leg when all was done.

We put Sandy in an outside pen with the intention of letting her go in a few days, but before we actually released her she developed a swelling in her good foot. We gave her an antibiotic, something usually done on a five-days-on, five-days-off sequence, but after the five days on, the swelling was no better and after the five days off it was worse. Tom Herbert supplied a more powerful antibiotic, but it had no effect. The foot still looked very bad, and I feared for Sandy. There was one spot that looked particularly ugly, and, as Tom was in bed with flu, I told Jean I was going to lance it.

'Do you know what you're doing?' she said.

'No' I said, 'but unless we do something we're going to lose this bird.'

I took my courage in my hands, made an incision, and out came huge quantities of pus and, eureka, a huge black thorn. Now we knew what we were dealing with, and though it took a lot of terramycin and a lot of squeezing and bathing, Sandy never looked back. When we eventually released her she went off like a rocket, as fit as a fiddle, and though she came back for food every day for a week or two we never feared for her.

While she had been in an outside pen getting ready for release, Glyn, easily identifiable by his exceptionally dark plumage, had been hovering around to chat her up. Not long after Sandy's release I saw the two of them sharing a rabbit at the roadside half a mile from the house. All the following summer and winter we saw them occasionally, and in the spring a neighbouring farmer, Ken Skippins, told us they had nested in a tree on his land, which was music to our ears because we knew Ken would never hurt them. In September, Glyn, Sandy, still with her white feather, and their three youngsters could be seen, high above us, every day. We pointed them out, very proudly, to anyone who visited Penfoel.

Once we had a peregrine for a fortnight. We have a friend who lives at Gwbert, near Cardigan, by the name of Griffiths. Known universally as Muffs, he divided his life between

accountancy and falconry. Lately, however, he has abandoned
accountancy to his son. Unlike some falconers we know, who
keep a sort of menagerie, Muffs only has one bird at a time,
which he gets at vast expense from places like South America.
His birds are royally treated. One day his little nephew, aged
about ten, was taking his spaniel for a walk when a peregrine
dived out of a bush and landed on the dog. That bird was lucky.
The boy knew what he had and could handle it. The peregrine
was starving and had an injured wing, and Muffs' nephew
carefully took it home. Muffs himself devoted weeks to caring
for it, then because he had to go away for a fortnight he left it
with us.

It was a female bird, called Droopy, by reason of her
hanging wing, a name we thought far too undignified for so
imperial a creature. We kept her on a block in an outside pen in
the daytime, and brought her in at night, the changeover taking
place with Droopy standing perfectly still on one's gloved left
fist. We couldn't help admiring the beauty and resilience of that
bird during the few days we had her and when, a month later,
we heard she died of a massive internal haemorrhage, we, and
Muffs, sorrowed greatly. Poor Droopy must have been injured
internally by the same accident that had damaged her wing.

Later in the same year, we heard that an eyrie of peregrines
near Llangranog had been raided and that the eyasses, the
babies, had been taken for sale to falconers less honourable
than our friends of that ilk. Arabs we were told, were paying
two or three thousand pounds for a peregrine in working order,
irrespective of age. We were furious about this, and when, the
following summer, Rosemary Bowen, the Secretary of the local
branch of the West Wales Naturalists' Trust asked us if we would
serve on a peregrine watch to prevent the same thing happening again, we jumped at the chance. We gave her a list of people
who had brought us birds for treatment during the preceding
couple of years who might be possible volunteers, and many of
them jumped at it too. We were all summoned to a briefing, on
site, shown where the nest was, and instructed that our role
was to prevent people from disturbing the birds by going too

close to the nest, and to observe anyone who tried to do so, and summon official help if they actually tried to get to the nest. Reaching the nest would have been quite an operation because the eyrie was about a hundred feet from the top of a three hundred foot cliff, whose face was made up of loose stones, not sound rock, but we were told that the police had just found three men in a van loaded with climbing gear, nets, live bait and all the other tackle necessary to get to the birds. Remembering how still our sparrowhawk had been in semi-darkness, our task suddenly became serious. The eyrie is overlooked by an observation post belonging to the RAE at Aberporth and we were able to use that for shelter and for access to a telephone.

People with a job to do during the day wardened from dawn to breakfast or from tea till dark, retired people or those with plenty of time watched in the day time, and there was a regular observer at night. Later on, members of the Hawk Trust and other ornithologists, who had come to the area on holiday, took their turn, and stayed on watch for days.

The peregrine watch was an excellent example of the greater joy one can get from watching a bird in the wild as a result of having treated a bird of the same species. A serious attempt was made to exterminate peregrines during the war because they killed carrier pigeons, and very many of the survivors died as a result of poisoning by pesticides during the 1950s. In the early sixties there were less than a hundred breeding pairs in the country. The numbers are increasing, but the need to protect isolated nests is obvious. But not many of the watchers had even seen a peregrine before they started looking after this eyrie, and hardly any of them had seen a peregrine close. The nearest one could get to this eyrie was three or four hundred yards but a closer approach would have been quite wrong, even if it had been physically possible, because of the disturbance it would have caused to the birds. At that distance, one cannot make out very much of the detail of a bird even with a good pair of glasses, but all we had to do was think back to Droopy to know just how a peregrine looks.

Jean and I reported for duty at 6.00 pm on a Tuesday. The

sense of responsibility was enormous. Our predecessors told us
that nothing untoward had happened, and that they had seen
no peregrines. The birds were waiting for us, we thought, and
we applied our binoculars to the scenery as if the future of
western civilization depended ·on our vigilance. After fifteen
minutes, during which no one appeared, let alone tried climbing down to the nest, we became aware of stonechats flitting
between the thistle heads, shags and cormorants all over the
bay below us, razorbills flying in and out of a cove in the cliff,
and a solitary chough passing overhead. We were on top of a
dome, five hundred feet high, two hundred yards from the sea,
and around us was some of the most breathtaking cliff scenery
in Wales. It was a perfect summer evening. Suddenly a bird
approached from the southwest, apparently making heavy
weather of it, with its tail down. As it passed about twenty
yards away we saw that it was the male peregrine, the tiercel,
carrying a dead pigeon. From then on we started to enjoy
ourselves.

We found a vantage point from which we could see the
eyrie and the cliffs round it much better than from the OP, and
we remained well covered in bracken so as not to disturb the
birds. We soon spotted the regular perches that the birds occupied, near, but not at, the nest. The tiercel was far more often to
be seen than the falcon, and we were not surprised to be told
later that three eggs had been laid, so the falcon would have
been sitting out of sight in the hole in the cliff face where she
had built her nest. Under these conditions she would be completely dependent on the tiercel for food, and we felt rather
sorry for her because her tiercel seemed an idle fellow, not at all
concerned about his duty to his spouse. He would fly off at mid
evening and return after an hour or so, perhaps bringing prey
with him, perhaps not. He never went direct to the eyrie, but
would sit on a perch fifty or a hundred feet away while the
falcon cried out to him. Very often she had no supper. We later
learned that this is quite normal practice amongst peregrines,
but it seemed a bit harsh.

In due course, we were assured that the eggs had hatched,

though how and from where anyone could have established this defeated me. We began to see far more of the falcon, and as the babies grew and their need for food increased, the activity of the parent birds increased, too, and our weekly stint as amateur wardens became more and more fascinating. The trouble was that we were too easily sidetracked by everything else around us.

It was hard to concentrate on the largely immobile peregrines when in the water below there were razorbills fishing, sometimes seals, oystercatchers on the rocks, and from a little cove a constant stream of shags and razorbills going to and from their nesting sites. Razorbills would swim along, half a dozen or a dozen in line abreast, all dipping their beaks underwater periodically, when quite suddenly, all of them. would dive so nearly simultaneously as to make it hard to believe they were not diving to a signal. From a height of a hundred feet or so they could be seen at quite considerable depths in the water, as could the seals, quietly but purposefully seeking the pollack which always feed in deepish water at the base of the cliffs. When the razorbills or the seals or whatever had moved out of sight we would return our attention to the cliff face. I have to confess that we were rather amateur compared to the Hawk Trust people themselves, who came with telescopes which would have enabled them to see peregrines in the next county, binoculars to watch them when they were in the air, cameras with telephoto lenses of unimaginable power, all with tripods to suit. If there was a peregrine in sight I was always impressed that they were sufficiently disciplined never to take their eyes off it.

Many gulls nested on ledges in the same cliff as the peregrines, apparently with mutual tolerance, because we never saw either species do anything nasty to the other, but there were quite a few pigeons about so it was rather surprising that we never saw either peregrine take a pigeon anywhere near the eyrie. Pigeons are the principal prey of peregrines, which take them by diving, or 'stooping' on them, while they are flying. It is said they reach speeds of up to 200 mph during their stoops and without being able to confirm or deny this figure, it is nonetheless a breathtaking sight. We see it occasionally on the farm at Penfoel, when a peregrine takes one of our doves or pigeons.

By July, the baby peregrines, the eyasses, can be seen at the eyrie, and once they are flying there is little point in maintaining watch, so wardening is abandoned. We rarely have any reason to believe that anything untoward happens during our vigil. Once I remember the evening was so foggy that I fancied I saw members of the ungodly lurking behind every gorse bush. I reflected that although I hadn't shot anyone since 1945 I still remembered how to do it. I only wished I had something with me to do it with. But of course the shadows were figments of my imagination, and all was well.

Much rarer even than the peregrine is the red kite, which lives in the hills to the east of us, in an area which starts about twenty miles away. There are only a couple of dozen pairs breeding. We've never had a sick one, though we may well do, one day. What a challenge that will be!

Another bird we've never treated is an eagle, and while I would never say I wouldn't treat one – we'll have a go at anything – it would require very different techniques. Near Solva, in Pembrokeshire, lives Gerald Summers, with his wife Imogen, seventeen dogs, an Imperial eagle, various other hawks, and Random, a golden eagle, a female. She won't have anything to do with Imogen but Gerald carries her on his fist, like any other trained hawk, and she's tame, or well trained, enough to fly free in the same way.

A golden eagle looks like a buzzard, but much bigger, I knew. I was amazed, however, when I first saw Random. She was as big as a swan. She was perching on a three inch log and her talons met round it, which makes them much bigger than a man's fingers. I thought of the strength of the various buzzards which had dug their talons into me and imagined with awe the power of those enormous claws. She held her wings well forward, like a wrestler's shoulders, and sat, massive and passive, like a bull in a good mood. She wasn't going to turn her head for any visitor, but I'm sure those great eyes missed nothing, under their beetling brows. One thing is quite certain – if we ever do have to handle an eagle, we'll need much heavier gloves than we've got!

7

Of Seals and Swans

In October 1976 we were asked by a friend in Borth to collect a
baby seal from her. Val Hughes is wonderful with birds and
treats many herself, but she didn't handle the seal so Hugh and I
drove over to Borth to fetch it. We took with us a plastic fish box
big enough to hold the seal, with a net on a frame by way of lid,
and – shades of Moses – we took gloves enough to tackle a
crocodile. With some trepidation we knocked on Val's door.

The seal, christened Flake, was loose in Val's kitchen,
but showed no aggressive tendencies whatever, and didn't
even resist being picked up. Because he was wheezing badly
we transferred him into our fish box, where he lay with a
seraphic smile on his face, and drove off at once to Tom Herbert,
in Aberaeron, so that Flake could have some antibiotic injections immediately. There, we all examined him carefully to be
sure he wasn't a gentle little common seal which had strayed
from its proper haunts but no, he was Atlantic Grey and no
mistake. We took him home.

He was beginning to moult, so he was ready to be fed on

fish, but until he had settled down a bit milk foods might be better than going through the battle of trying to give him fish. We therefore slid a length of quarter-inch plastic tube down his throat, and pumped half a pint of glucose and Complan direct into his stomach. He was asleep in a moment in his box, well wrapped up in blankets. He hardly moved during the night, nor during the next day, and we gave him glucose and Complan every couple of hours. At eleven o' clock we went to give him his last feed before we went to bed, but just before leaving him, his breathing got worse. Quite suddenly, he was not just wheezing, but gasping for breath, and Jean rang Tom Herbert, who was in bed.

While she was on the phone Flake stopped breathing altogether. I yelled out to Jean to tell Tom what had happened. I picked Flake up, listened to his chest, found his heart was still beating, and started artificial respiration. I kept this up until Tom arrived at about 11.45 pm, but just as we heard the car arriving Flake's heart stopped. I couldn't help thinking of the television hospital programmes wherein the blip on the oscilloscope gets slower and smaller until only a straight line remains. Tom came charging in, his wife with him, and I had to apologize for yanking them out of bed for nothing. Flake was dead. But being the sort of people they are, Tom and Jackie merely said they were deeply sorry that they hadn't arrived sooner. I think they knew before they got out of bed that Flake hadn't much chance. But Tom, a vet in a million, would never have let the knowledge stop him coming out to visit.

Flake's gentleness had been the result of weakness, not of a kind disposition, and I had a dreadful feeling that I had got the plastic tube into his lungs, not his stomach. If he was as weak as all that, I reasoned, maybe his reflexes would have failed to react and, if so, I had drowned him. The next morning I took him to the veterinary investigation lab, in Aberystwyth, where they opened him up and showed me his lungs, full of fluid but not full of milk. I was relieved that lung congestion had killed him, not my feeding, and the lab showed me the strength of the valve which closes off the wind pipe and assured me that the chances of ever getting a pipe past it were exceedingly remote and that, however weak Flake was, his reaction, if it had happened, would have been explosive. Somewhat comforted I went to work.

A couple of days later about seven in the evening, we heard of another stranded baby seal. Henry Jones of Aberarth, telephoned to say that during the afternoon he had seen a baby seal on the beach near the village. He had kept his distance, in order not to worry it, but he was concerned about it and had gone out again at six to see if it was still there. As it hadn't moved he thought we ought to take a look at it. So off we went, and he led us to it, lying quietly on the shingle.

By this time we had had some instruction in respect of seal behaviour and tried out what we had been told. A man must look enormous to a baby seal, whose eye level is only about four inches above the ground, so we crawled up to it accordingly, making gentle howling noises containing, or so we had been told, the essential notes of a mother seal's call. Mr Jones must have thought we were crazy, but it worked. The little seal relaxed completely and we got it into our fish box and put it in the car with no trouble. In the silence of the car, the baby's breathing was like a leaky steam engine. Quite obviously, it was in urgent need of antibiotics. That meant taking it to the vet.

'We can't do it,' I said. 'It's nine o'clock on Saturday night. Every man has a right to a bit of peace sometimes.'

'We'll have to,' said Jean. 'Tom won't thank us for leaving him in peace if this fellow dies as well.'

Jean was right but we tossed up to decide who should ring Tom's bell. We stood by the door, the box with the seal in it between us, and I felt like a small boy brought to the man whose apples I had been stealing.

'I'm afraid we've got another seal,' I said, as Tom opened the door. 'Its breathing is terrible.'

I got no further.

'Jackie,' Tom yelled to his wife, 'another seal,' and in seconds he was examining the little scrap in the surgery and administering a massive antibiotic injection to deal with lung congestion – tylan, this time, not penicillin, having memories of Moses' allergy. We found that for a change we had a little lady seal. Jackie photographed her from all angles, and we decided to call her Ripple.

As we took her home, we reflected that as she was about the same size as Moses, and bigger and stronger than Flake, we stood a good chance of saving her. The first item on the agenda, obviously, was to feed her, and with some dismay I realized that this meant a return to the welding gloves and getting crunched four times a day. As I put on my gloves and my waterproof trousers, the memories came flooding back. Mo had never caused us any real injury, but we'd certainly used a lot of Savlon and sticking plaster as a result of his efforts. I therefore approached Ripple very carefully, at floor level, crooning gently as I did so. To my amazement I put my hands on her neck without a snap. I opened her mouth and Jean quickly pushed a fish down her throat. We gave her three or four more fish quite easily, she didn't snap when I let her go, we put her in her box, with a blanket, switched the infra-red lamp on, and she was asleep in a minute.

The next day I fed her myself, with only one hand gloved, pushing the fish down with the second and third fingers of the other, and after five days she was taking fish from Jean's hand and swallowing them on her own. Three days later she was picking them up by herself. Ken Jones had been quite right. We were lucky to have had a rogue to start with.

Unlike Moses, Ripple was quite uninterested in little fish like sprats; instead she shovelled up mackerel and herring like a JCB on full throttle. This was good, because little Ripple was actually very sick. It was weeks before she would breathe properly, and in addition to her lung congestion she had an umbilical ulcer. This is very common in baby seals, and follows from the fact that during the first two weeks of a baby seal's life, during which it does not normally go into water, it is dragging itself over rocks that are covered with its own and other seals' droppings. Infection starts with sepsis on the surface, and an ulcer forms which first eats away the seal's liver and finally causes peritonitis, which is usually fatal. Fortunately we had caught Ripple's ulcer in time and it responded to antibiotics; by the end of November all that remained was a purple stain from the terramycin aerosol we had been using to treat it.

Once she was fit, Ripple began to show her personal idiosyncrasies, just like Moses had done. As befitted a lady, she was far more delicate than he had been, and took to filleting her fish. She would hold a herring or mackerel by the head, using her teeth, insert one or two claws of her front flipper into its gills, rip away one flank of the fish, eat it, and then rip away the other. She would leave the head, backbone and tail as clean as any cat. The trouble was, this made dosing very difficult, which could have been serious, because all marine mammals in captivity are given daily doses of vitamins to make up for those destroyed when fish is frozen. We got over this by doping every fish until she swallowed one whole.

Ripple carried her little blanket with her wherever she went, except in the tank, and, although she would push hard with her nose against my fist if I offered it to her, like Mo did, she was no more anxious to have her head stroked or her tummy rubbed than he was. Christmas came, and we gave her a tiny tree of her own, but by that time we had acquired some other patients.

One of our friends, Bernice Jones, the member for Wales of the Council of the RSPCA, lives in Gwent where she presides over a big home for stray and unwanted cats and dogs, and is very successful in finding homes for them. During that December she found two swans in her shelter. They had flown into a lagoon of waste oil in the Spencer steel works at Llanwern near Newport, and had been brought in by two security men who had found them. Bernice asked us if we could do anything for them and of course we said we'd try. An RSPCA van brought them halfway and we duly picked them up.

The two swans sat alongside each other in the back of the van, their necks interwined. They were covered head to foot, every feather soaked, with black, sticky, smelly, oil. It was just as well that I had taken the precaution of covering the back seat of the car with plenty of newspaper and an old curtain. I picked up the female of the pair, the pen, but it was very difficult to separate its neck from that of its mate, so firmly were they twisted.

I know that swans mate for life and show great loyalty to their mates, but nothing had prepared me for the pitiful, despairing little cries that that swan made when she was separated from her spouse. I dived back to the van to fetch the cob, which was making the same pitiful sounds. He was much lighter than the pen, and seemed to be having difficulty holding up his head. As soon as I put him down by the pen, she curled her neck round his, and lifted his head with hers. If it had not been obvious that action was called for if we were to save the swans, Jean and I would have wept right there by the roadside.

Jean always comes prepared for anything on these occasions and now she produced a bowl of bread, glucose, water and vitamin B12. At first neither swan showed any interest, so Jean held the bowl up and gently dipped their bills in it. First one, then the other began nibbling her fingers, they started drinking the water, slowly at first and, after a minute or so, greedily, and soon they'd emptied the bowl, and eaten a quarter of the loaf. I drove off. Very soon Jean said she thought they wanted more so I stopped the car and she offered them another full bowl. Most of that went down, too, and I drove off again. Jean spent the rest of the longer-than-usual journey of one and a half hours, leaning over the back of her seat to feed our feathered friends in the back. Altogether they took in one big loaf and a gallon of water between them.

We took our swans into the kitchen when we got home, and gave them a good fill of concentrated glucose and Complan, laced with antibiotics. They sat together, by the Rayburn while we considered what to do next. Swans are not accustomed to being soaked in oil, to being carted about in motor cars, to being handled by people, nor sitting in kitchens, so ours could be assumed to be in a state of stress. We couldn't very well put them in the bird room because we had no pens big enough for them, so they would have to be loose on the floor, and Ripple was already in occupation of that. She was likely to set up even more stress in the birds. It would have been nice to let them rest for a day or two before trying to clean them up, but it was at least arguable that their filthy condition was upsetting them more than anything else. It was essential to stop them preening, and so ingesting more of the filthy oil which covered them, but it was difficult to fit effective ponchos on them. A poncho works well on a bird with an upright stance like a guillemot but, as we discovered, not on a bird with an almost level back like a swan. The poncho is round its neck like a scarf in no time. Se we decided instead to give them an immediate wash, a quick one, to get the bulk of the oil off, which would at least eliminate the smell and fumes of the oil and perhaps restore their self-respect a bit.

We decided to call them Peter and Wendy, and took them upstairs. It was then we began to realize just how big a swan is. When carried, it assumed the same attitude it would in flight, that is with its neck fully extended forward. Its reach is fantastic. It wasn't the first doorway that caused problems. The tricky part was to align the bird at each doorway so that one could get its head through the next.

Peter and Wendy would not go in the bath in line. They overlapped by a foot in the middle. We ran eight inches of water in the bath and put two large bottles of Co-op green in. While the bath was filling, we put each bird on the bathroom scales. Wendy was well up to weight at twenty-two pounds, but Peter only weighed twelve.

Jean knelt down and started washing Peter, who immediately wrapped his neck round hers, and when I got down to do Wendy she wrapped hers round mine also. We gently soaked the two birds in the usual way and got an enormous quantity of filth off them. We took our time about it, in order not to worry them, but decided against giving them a second wash despite the fact they seemed beautifully relaxed; one can never be sure whether quiet behaviour in birds indicates relaxation or extreme weakness. We dried the birds, fan heaters for the big areas, Jean's hair drier for the tricky bits, and though there was still some dirt on them it did not come off easily, so as they were not likely to get much more off however hard they preened, we fed them again and went to bed, leaving them in the kitchen but well away from the heat. They were both making bubbling sounds when they breathed, so it was clear we musn't let them get too cold; but as they had never been indoors before being too warm wouldn't do them much good either. We hoped we'd got it right.

Peter seemed a little stronger the following morning. He was holding his head up better, and Wendy wasn't propping him up so much. I went to the office feeling quite hopeful, but during the afternoon Jean heard Wendy crying very gently and went to see what was wrong, only to find her trying to lift Peter's head. He was, quite suddenly, too weak to hold it up himself. His breathing was much worse, so Jean sat on the floor, cradled him on her lap and held his head up. Wendy sat alongside and wrapped her neck around his, and there they all remained until Peter died, about an hour later. When I got home, about half-past five, Wendy was still trying to revive him, making her pitiful little cry, and Jean was in tears, too. Wendy stayed by Peter's side all night, and it was only with some difficulty that I managed to persuade her to release his body the next morning so that I could take him away for a post-mortem. Poor Peter, his lungs were full of fluid. He must have been very sick even before he landed in the oil.

Wendy herself was very ill for the next three days. She ate nothing on her own but we kept her going with Complan and glucose squirted gently down her throat. A swan's normal food is green stuff – water weed, grass, etc – and they graze like sheep. Wendy wouldn't touch grass for four days, but then she ate a lettuce and started again on grass. Over Christmas, which was the tenth day after she came to us, Wendy seemed to be really fit, but on 28 December she went off her food once more, on the 30th she was reluctant to stand up, and on New Year's Eve she died. The vet lab said it was aspergillosis, and I'm sure they were right, but I'm also sure that losing Peter triggered it off. It was our first experience of what 'mating for life' means in non-human terms.

During the brief sojourn of Wendy and Peter, we had derived much comfort – and we needed it – by watching Ripple. She had not been knocked about like Moses, so her fur was not covered in scars as his had been. Also, and this is highly unusual in grey seals, her coat was a uniform pale-fawn in colour, and when it was dry it looked like sable. She was a real picture, and quite early in the New Year when she was as fat as butter our thoughts turned to returning her to the sea. Once again, the question arose where to send her.

There is a little beach in north Pembrokeshire, between Newport and the Teifi, where quite large numbers of seals haul out every spring to moult. Only the adults actually moult, but there are always plenty of youngsters about as well. The difficulty of finding congenial company for our baby would be solved by releasing her near this spot, but it posed another problem – the higher the number of seals in any location, the greater the pressure of the local foodstocks. Would Ripple find enough food for herself? On balance, we decided it was worth that risk, because it meant that we could release Ripple at any time the weather was not too rough. We had waited nearly a month for the firm location of a bunch of youngsters for Moses to join, and we had not liked that delay at all. Indeed as I said earlier, we have often noticed a serious deterioration in birds in our care whose condition has been perfect but whose release has been delayed, say, by bad weather. Moses had gone off his food during that month and had gazed out of the window all the time instead of fooling about as usual. He had been all right in the end but a longer delay might have seriously upset him. We feel sure that birds and seals know when they are ready to depart and will gain nothing by being kept longer.

Arrangements were made accordingly. On Tuesday Ripple was to have a final booster of antibiotics and B12, on Wednesday a dose of cod-liver oil, and on Thursday she was to go back. Tom Herbert came over to give the injections and Ripple, with perfect manners, allowed Jean to hold her while he did it. As he pushed the plunger, though, Ripple shot like a rocket out of Jean's hands, straight into the tank, where she sat in the

1 Jean with Princess Dot, *p.107*

2 William and Princess Dot, clean at last, *p.108*

3 A badly oiled razorbill   4 A lightly oiled razorbill

5 Washing an oiled razorbill

6 Rinsing a razorbill

7 A clean razorbill

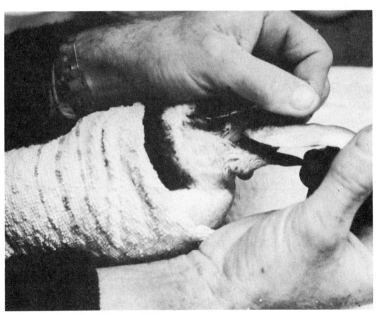

8 Force-feeding a razorbill

9 Applying hand cleanser to a guillemot

10 Washing a guillemot

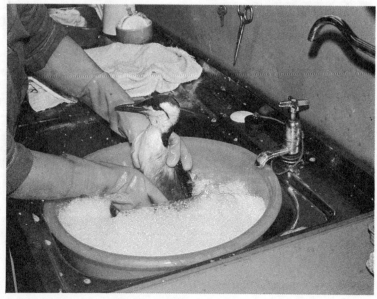

furthest corner. She clapped her flippers, beat her chest and chattered away like mad. Tom made a very charming little speech, apologizing if he'd hurt her and explaining it was all for her good, and she splashed half the tank over him. He'd got the antibiotic into her but there was no way of getting at her again for the B12. I volunteered to do that the next day.

The dose of cod-liver oil called for the tube-down-the-throat treatment, so I put on the heavy gloves and got started. I slipped the soft plastic tube down with the greatest of ease, and so quiet was Ripple that I felt quite ashamed of wearing the gloves. Jean came along with a big syringe with the cod liver oil in it, stuck it in the tube and slowly squirted it in. Ripple never moved. I was murmuring endearing expressions to her, naturally, while all this was going on. I pulled the tube away, just as Jean turned from the work-top with the B12 injection ready, a syringe with a needle in it. Ripple went mad. She charged away from me, but not before she had got in two quick snaps at my left hand and really mangled my thumb and first finger through two layers of chrome treated horsehide. She never did get the B12 injection.

The next day, by courtesy of the National Park wardens, we took her to Ceibwr, the nearest beach to the haul-out, which is not accessible from the land. Meeting us were Stephen Evans of the Nature Conservancy Council, Margaret Patterson, Chairman of the West Wales Naturalists Trust, and Nona Rees – Ripple was to have a splendid send-off.

As Ripple had no obvious identifying marks like Moses, we thought hard to find a way of marking her. The terramycin aerosol we had used on her umbilicus contained gentian violet, and the purple stain we had thus applied in October was still clearly visible at Christmas. So we released her with a neat purple stripe down her back. We put her gently in the sea and away she went. For half an hour she explored the little bay, then swam out into the open sea. As she did so, two other youngsters appeared, and the three went off together, in the right direction.

The following Sunday we went to the haul-out, to find 139 youngsters. Every one was lying on its back, flippers crossed, the picture of contentment, but there was no purple stripe in sight. We never saw Ripple again, but since we'd been told that Moses was bigger and fatter than his contemporaries who had spent their first winter in the wild, and since Ripple was as big as Mo had been, we weren't worried for her safety.

We reflected on the fact that whereas most people regard swans as dangerous and aggressive creatures, but think that seals are cuddly and gentle, our experience had been the reserse. No bird we had ever treated had been as docile as Wendy and Peter but whenever we talked of the seal's apparent liking for human blood no one would believe us. Heaven knows, we never exaggerated in our accounts of Mo's behaviour, and little Flake had only been as gentle as a lamb because he had been so ill. We wondered whether our swans had been too ill to behave naturally. How would healthy swans behave?

We found out in June. Two more swans flew into the steelworks lagoon of oil, but this time everyone knew what to do with them and they were on their way to us the same day. When I picked them up each swan was already in a feed bag, the neck of which was tied round the base of the swan's neck. That's a sound idea, I thought, they won't get those off, so they can't preen and ingest a lot of oil. Quite happily I transferred the two birds to the car. They were just as docile as Peter and Wendy had been, and just as oily, but this time the oil was brown.

But there was something in the look of the two great birds that I didn't like, although I couldn't actually see anything wrong. I stroked the neck of one, and finally on an impulse, felt its bill, which was hot. If a hot bill indicated a high blood temperature in a gannet it probably meant the same for a swan. I undid the tie at the neck of the bag enclosing the bird's body and immediately I knew why. The heat inside was fantastic. So I slit the bag from end to end and a great cloud of oily vapour arose, and the poor bird stood up, oil dripping off it. There must have been a pint of the stuff in the bag. I cut the other bird free, threw the bags into a rubbish bin and drove off with all the windows of the car open to cool the birds down. I don't think they would have survived another hour in those bags.

After a few miles I stopped and Jean offered them water-soaked bread as she had with Peter and Wendy. They gravely dipped their bills in the bowl, ate a little, and politely but firmly refused more. I drove home, and we brought them into the house. They were nothing like as attached to each other as Peter and Wendy had been, so we felt they were not a mated pair. We were not too sorry in a way, for Peter and Wendy's mutual attachment had carried emotional overtones which were still ringing round the house.

We called these two William and Mary and, not being constrained this time to treat them together, washed them separately. An enormous amount of oil came off them but we recognized that we had a marathon cleaning job on our hands and didn't attempt to get them completely clean that evening. The birds were well up to weight and seemed fit, but there is a limit to any bird's endurance and it was better to leave the last of the oil for another day. They were not quite white after we dried them, but they were not far off.

They stayed in the kitchen overnight, the bird room being rather full, and we put them in a makeshift pen outside the next day. As soon as I had gone to work, Jean had a phone message to say a third swan needed treatment. I was tied up at the office, so Bill Stratford and his wife went to fetch it and we called it Princess Dot, after Dot Stratford. Jean and I washed her when I finally got home in the late evening.

Our work on William and Mary was reasonably thorough, but the result turned out to be very disappointing. The day after we washed them they looked almost as bad as when they came in. Princess Dot was the same. We washed them all again, and they looked fine, but once more they were reddish brown all over by the following morning. Evidently, we were not getting to the base of the feathers, and there was enough oil remaining there to soak back to the outside within twelve hours of washing. We washed them again, with more care, but the same thing happened. At the seventh wash, the water was not discoloured at all, so we had obviously got very little, if any, oil off in the wash, yet the reddish-brown stain was back all over each bird the next morning. We had realized with Peter and Wendy that the thickness and density of a swan's plumage put it in a class apart from every other bird we had washed, but it now seemed it was too dense for the washing process which worked on the other birds. We couldn't devise any better way of washing them, so we would have to wait for them to moult and grow new feathers, something which should take place round about September. We didn't mind keeping them the six weeks or so that was necessary, but we were afraid that they might develop some infection in captivity, or, like the scoters, that their moult might go all wrong in unnatural surroundings. We had to keep them constrained because they were perfectly capable of flight but if they had landed in water, they would quite certainly sink. A bird's feathers, dry, can weigh as much as his skeleton; wet, they can weigh as much as the bird.

The first thing was to build a fox-proof pen so that the three swans could live out of doors. Until it was ready we had the birds in a makeshift pen on the lawn during the day but we were afraid to leave them out at night. Each night and morning there was a beautiful little procession, William, Mary and Princess Dot, always in that order, paddling on their enormous feet from kitchen to pen or back. They were alright in the kitchen at night, because the Rayburn was out, but we used to cover the floor with newspaper. Early morning, all three would silently paddle over to the sink while the soiled paper near the door was changed, then paddle back to the clean paper while the same was done by the sink. The kitchen table is nearly three feet high, and one of the birds drank Hugh's coffee one morning without spilling the cup, which rather shows how far a swan can reach.

We wanted advice on how to treat our trio, to keep them fit and ensure that they moulted properly, so, as usual, we asked Peter Davies. He is part of the Institute for Terrestial Ecology, and is doing research into that rarest of British birds, the red kite. His knowledge of birds is equalled only by his willingness to pass it on. He felt the birds should be fine in their pen, and, with much more conviction than we had, that William, Mary and Princess Dot had been correctly named by sex. He wasn't too sure about the ideal diet so I checked with Michael Lubbock of Slimbridge who recommended soaked bread, with vitamin supplements, Winalot for protein, and lettuce. We had two acres of lettuce outside, out of which we'd hoped to make a fortune, but which no one wanted to buy, so the swans ate four huge ones each every day.

The moult duly arrived and went according to nature. Swans moult all their feathers together, so we must have had 75,000 feathers loose in the pen. I've seen burst feather mattresses which made less mess, but the birds came up like the driven snow.

As soon as it was over, we took them to Peter Moss, of the Coedmor Wildlife Park near Cardigan, who lives at Rosehill farm which borders on the River Teifi. There are about twenty pairs of swans on the river, between Coedmor and the sea. In due time, our little trio made up their own minds, and they walked determinedly to the river. We had marked them with coloured rings, and the following summer two of them set up house on a little island in Peter's marsh and raised a family.

We were delighted about this, naturally. Every one likes to feel successful, but we still had a real regret that we had not handled a fit, live, wild swan. Everyone, except us, was convinced that swans were aggressive and dangerous creatures. Years ago, when our children were small they were feeding two swans on the river in Haverfordwest, offering them sliced bread, slice by slice. Those birds were accustomed to people and and would eat a slice up to the children's fingers. None of us ever got bitten, but we almost started a riot. An extraordinary number of people photographed the children doing something they clearly regarded as fantastic, and quite a few berated us for exposing them to such danger. The fuss was such that Jean and I wondered whether all the people with cameras really wanted pictures of children feeding swans or whether they were secretly hoping to see swans eating children. Finally one woman went off sounding like a Valkyrie to fetch the police and the NSPCC, but we felt that discretion was the better part of valour, so we pushed off before she came back.

When we first had William and Mary and Princess Dot, and I was building the pen for them, a man called to see me – about something else altogether.

'Swans,' he said, when he heard. 'In the house? Don't you know a swan can break a man's arm?'

Now I've often heard this tale, and it may even have happened, but I'm quite certain that I could more easily hurt a swan than be hurt by one, and said so. I pointed out how gentle the birds actually are, and invited him to look at them. He wouldn't even come to the hatch to see them, let alone the kitchen door. Then he noticed that my hand was badly scratched, the result of cutting the mesh wire for the pen, and he asked what had happened. When I told him, he pointed out that this injury was a direct result of having swans about the place, and departed happily.

Our next swan was Old Bill, a venerable cob from a steel works pond in Llanelli, who – sickeningly – had been beaten on the head by vandals and had been made blind for life. He became a permanent resident. We always try to get our patients back to the wild but we couldn't push Old Bill out. He needs a bit of protection, bless him. But he wasn't a real wild swan either.

Neither was Nuala, our next intake of the species, who, in her first year had flown into something and stripped all the muscles and tendons of the top bone of her left wing. Tom Herbert managed to save the injured wing but she will never be able to fly again, so she is still with us, too. As I've said, it's wholly against our principles to keep any bird here, but she could get nowhere in the wild, and she and old Bill are lovely together.

It was a load of fishing line, that scourge of the water bird, that enabled me finally to catch a perfectly healthy swan. A summer visitor rang to say there was a swan with fishing line all over its head and bill on the river bank, midway between Cardigan and Gwbert. Jean told the visitor to offer the swan a slice of bread and, when it came close enough to take it, catch the bird and get the line off it. If he couldn't get the line off, she advised, take it to a vet in Cardigan, who would. She had doubts as to the visitor's competence in the matter so she rang Muffs, our falconer friend, who lives not far away, and asked him to go over and help.

The swan came right up to them to get the bread, Muffs told us afterwards, and then turned, presenting the visitor with the perfect chance to catch it, which he made no attempt to take.

'It hissed at me,' he said.

Muffs comment was brief and to the point. 'Bloody visitors.'

Then he organized half the parish to help him, the following afternoon. He wasn't going to lose the bird a second time, and zero hour was four o'clock. I had to go to Cardigan myself that day and having a minute to spare at about two, went to try to see this unhappy swan. I soon found a swan, on its own, in the right place more or less, and approached it very slowly to make sure. It was the one, alright, nylon wrapped around its head and bill, and trailing miles behind it.

I wished that I had some bread with me, and I was just wondering whether to go and get some or leave it to Muffs, when I found I wasn't alone. Alongside me was Robert Shehan, known to his friends as Bodo, who came, he told me, every day, at that time, to feed the swan. He had been thinking of catching it, but was afraid of making a mess of the job and hurting it.

It came right up to us and, without any bother, I took its head in one hand and put my other arm round its body. I acknowledge that if you get hold of a swan's head but miss his wings, and you are alone, you have problems, but quite apparently it's not difficult to get hold of a swan if you know what to do – on land, anyway.

This one had swallowed a good deal of line, and gentle pulling wouldn't free it, so we popped it in the well behind the front passenger's seat of my car and sought veterinary help in Cardigan. Bodo and I sat in the surgery waiting room, with the swan, wrapped in an enormous, tattered curtain I carry in the car for this sort of thing. It was as good as gold, not moving at all, but it did spot a chihuahua sitting on a lady's lap about six feet away and hissed quietly for a moment. The chihuahua shot under its owner's coat. Evidently, other creatures besides humans regard swans as dangerous.

Sitting in the waiting room, my spirits began to droop. What if our feathered friend was full of hooks they wouldn't be able to release, and had to be put down? There had been an enormous mass of line dangling from his bill, but there had been no hooks on that. We'd looked most carefully. He'd taken the bait, I reflected miserably, hook and all, and swallowed it, and when he departed rapidly, as he most certainly would do, the line had parted at the reel. It was just as well we hadn't long to wait.

We were called into the treatment room by the vet on duty, Adrian Batten, who was not in the least concerned about being brought a swan. From his manner, he might have treated swans every day. Perhaps he did. My spirits rose. Feeling gently with his fingers he found three hard lumps in the bird's neck, any of which might have contained a hook.

'Not to worry,' he said. 'If he's got a hook stuck I'll soon get it out but I want to be sure first.'

He cut the line, then cut a length of soft plastic tube to match the swan's neck, threaded it on the line, and worked it very gently down its throat. It passed the first lump – no hook there. It passed the second, then the third. Very gently, Adrian withdrew the tube, and all the line came with it. No hook, no injury. He applied a purple stripe, as we had done on Ripple, on the swan's back and up its neck, and the job was done.

Bodo and I thanked everyone in sight, several times, and we took our swan back where we'd found it. Off it went, with a monumental sore throat no doubt, but otherwise unhurt. I went to tell Muffs what we'd done so that he could stand down his faithful band, and to this day I don't know whether he was pleased or sorry.

I reflected, as I have done hundreds of times, that treating sick birds and animals is great fun when it works, as it had done that day, beyond question. That swan had been saved simply because I, having handled swans before, knew how to catch it. I wondered how many other birds had died because people, though caring and willing, had not felt able to catch them and treat them or take them for treatment. For once, however, the thought didn't depress me. I felt great.

There is one snag about treating swans, though, which I haven't yet mentioned. They don't always come unaccompanied. Nuala, in particular, was rich in fellow-travellers. It was a young lady called Nuala who had told us about the swan with the bad wing, on the river Teifi in the village of Llechryd, near Cardigan. When I got there, Nuala the girl and Nuala the swan were sitting eyeball to eyeball in a field by the river, girl feeding swan. After getting the swan into the car, Nuala and I sat chatting on a low wall bordering the main road in the village. After a while, I asked her if she could find a spider or something, which was tickling my hair, and she started looking for it.

'It's not a spider,' she said, 'it's a little wriggly thing,' and she trod on it. A moment later, 'I think there's another one there,' I said. 'Oh, yes' she said, 'and another.' Then she said, 'My hair's itching now.'

And in a second, there we were, like a couple of chimps, preening each other by the roadside, beyond the decencies.

The rug I had put over the bird was alive with 'little wriggly things', which Jean finally identified as a kind of louse which affects birds, and we sprayed the car liberally with insect killer. We took the swan to Tom Herbert, sitting on a towel on Jean's lap, and all the way, in both directions, Jean was catching these insects on Nuala the swan's neck and head, and dropping them through the car window. Eventually we got hold of a suitable insect killer to apply to the bird and the lice were no more.

But I spent most of the evening having Jean pulling the things off me, and the rest of it in the bath. I felt dirty for a week. Jean never had one on her. There's equality for you.

8

Trouble in the Autumn

Treating oiled birds may be fun when it works, but it can also be a very demanding pursuit. When we have a big rush, I take a week's leave, we eat ploughman's lunches or bacon and eggs instead of a roast, and make major inroads on our friends' time as well as our own. This situation is fortunately quite rare, but there is a steady succession of oiled birds for treatment, two or three at a time, all the year round.

I said earlier that a bird's plumage will hold water equal to the bird's own weight, so obviously no bird that has become waterlogged has a hope of flying. For a contaminated bird to get ashore it must either take off immediately, before it is badly waterlogged, or be blown ashore. We once stood by for a week while 1500 helpless, oiled auks were blown first towards, then away from the Pembrokeshire coast, while efforts to net them from boats and from helicopters failed completely. They all drowned in the end.

We get very few oiled birds during the breeding season, presumably because in the inshore waters to which their parental duties restrict them, there is very little oil on the water. We get very few in midwinter, too, presumably because at that time the birds are too far out to sea to be able to reach land in time. It is mostly during spring and autumn that they come in, when they are far enough out at sea to be vulnerable to oil dumped by ships cleaning their tanks, but near enough to land for some at least to get to the shore. I'm referring here, of course, to the auks, the razorbills and guillemots, which are the birds principally affected by oiling.

All tankers have to wash their tanks as soon as possible after discharging cargo, and most of them do so at sea, as near as possible to the port of discharge. Some adopt what is known as the load-on-top system, in which the washings are retained in the ship and only the water discharged, but the load-on-top method, of course, is rather more expensive. The amount of oil actually discharged is very small, generally, oil being so very valuable, but it spreads very quickly over the water surface. It degrades by oxidation, particularly if the sea is choppy, and it soon disappears altogether, but until it has gone it is disastrous to any bird which lands in it.

Seals are born mostly in the month of September, but quite a few arrive in August or October. Orphaned, or lost, or sick seals, seem to hang on until they are a month or so old before they haul out onto a beach with people on it, and it is only then that one can see how much treatment they need. In the water a sick seal will soon lose what body fat it has, to keep its metabolism going, and then hypothermia sets in. Ashore, it will lose its fat much more slowly, but since it cannot feed ashore it will not last long there either. An underweight baby seal that finishes up on a beach is doomed unless someone can help it.

October, then, is likely to be our big month, but September and November are close behind. Moses and Ripple had taught us many things, among them that there was no way we could properly look after oiled birds and a seal at the same time. Ripple's behaviour had been fine, but Moses' predeliction for popping out from nowhere and biting one's ankle would have made treating birds in the same room an occupation like swimming in a swamp full of crocodiles. The real problem is that our indoor tank cannot be used by both seals and birds. A seal here, just as in the wild, will spend a lot of its time in the water and in a small tank the water soon gets dirty. Quite apart from the seal defecating in it, it will be full of bits of fish and if the seal is being fed mackerel or herring, there will be an oily film on the surface. It is essential for a bird that has been washed, rinsed and dried to spend as much time as possible preening itself, and it will only do this if it is in and out of water constantly. But the water must be clean, since the slightest contamination will destroy the bird's waterproofing in no time. One bird can play in our tank all day without trouble and without changing the water. Three or four cannot, so we have a constant flow arrangement with an outfall over a weir so that the surface film is always being drawn off.

Outside accommodation is less useful than it appears at first glance in this connection. We have an outside pen, about twelve feet by nine, with a tank in the floor. One end has a little building to provide shelter if it is necessary, one side is a simulated cliff with holes and ledges for birds to hide in or perch on, each bird to its taste. It was intended for the rehabilitation of birds before release, and it is fine for that purpose, but a bird has to be properly waterproofed before it is put outside, particularly in cold weather. Equally, the great outdoors is no place for an un-insulated baby seal in the winter, certainly not one with lung congestion. Water in a tank would be far colder than the sea.

We had been lucky in having no oiled birds at the same time as Moses. In 1975 we had lots of birds, but no seal. Our only problem coincident with Ripple had been the swans, Peter and Wendy. We wondered what the autumn of 1977 would bring.

Trouble started early that year. On 9th September, a Friday, we started hearing that there were oiled birds on the Pembrokeshire beaches, and the next day we heard they were being collected. They were covered, we were told, in heavy fuel oil. By the Sunday we had taken delivery of twenty-one guillemots, two shearwaters, one first-year gannet and one immature herring gull.

The shearwaters had rubbed their breasts on something with oil on it and were only very slightly affected. The herring gull had oil only on its tail and its wing tips. But the rest were covered, up to the plimsoll line, in heavy fuel oil. I knew that this was a very viscous substance at atmospheric temperature and that it had to be heated to make it thin enough to be pumped to the boiler or whatever in which it was to be burnt, but the stuff on these birds was hard. We had met crude oil in all stages, depending on the port of origin and the time it had been exposed, from thin liquid to sticky stuff that barely came off on our fingers, but we had never seen anything like this. The residue from crude oil, after everything else has been distilled off is bitumen, the black stuff used to stick roads together. Tar is not used for this now, it is far too valuable for making aspirins and nylons and so on. The stuff on these birds was bitumen, and since most of them had sand and little pebbles stuck on them, too, it looked like small areas of road surface, and just as hard.

It is normal to wrap a bird in a poncho or slide it into a length cut out of a nylon stocking to prevent it preening, and the guillemots were mostly dressed up in one of these ways, but some genius had put six of them into the leg portion of old socks. These were very tight, so we cut the socks off, but by Monday, all six birds had died, so we rang everyone who was collecting birds to say don't use old socks. Their deaths were upsetting but it gave us a chance to experiment on them without doing any harm. We found that a solution of washing-up liquid wouldn't touch the bitumen, so we tried it neat. Again it simply flowed off. We liberally soaked one of the dead birds and left it in a dish with detergent in it, but even after a couple of hours the bitumen was as hard as when we started. Washing-up liquid wasn't good enough for the job, evidently, which worried us because the only published work on cleaning oiled birds was the Newcastle recommendations and the only cleaning agent recommended *was* cheap washing-up liquid.

Hand cleansers are generally not suitable for the job

because many of them incorporate barrier creams which are necessarily insoluble and which are very difficult to wash off. That left solvents, and we shuddered at the prospect. To remove the bitumen with a solvent meant immersing the bird in the stuff, and agitating the feathers until it was all dissolved, then rinsing the bird in a second wash or even a third, until no trace of bitumen remained. The last rinse would have to be in perfectly clean solvent, and, if the solvent was perfectly clean itself – that is, it had no ingredients which would deposit themselves on the bird when it evaporated – it should have the bird clean and waterproof. We couldn't really believe that this would work, and even if it did it would require a gallon of fresh solvent for every guillemot and far more for each gannet.

I rang Esso Petroleum at Milford Haven for some suggestions and recommendations about solvents. The best one, they said would be medium virgin naphtha, but unfortunately they didn't have any. Then I had a brainwave. Would toluene be any good, I asked, because I knew I had some knocking about the house? Esso said it would certainly dissolve the bitumen and leave no residue when it evaporated, but they hadn't suggested it because it was slightly carcinogenic. But they added that one would have to swim in it for weeks before it would have any really harmful effects, so we decided immediately to try it on a dead bird.

It soon dissolved the bitumen, but as my stock was only one gallon there wasn't enough to wash a bird all over so I still didn't know whether it would get a live bird properly clean. There was plenty to worry about without that, anyway. By bedtime on Monday, eight of the guillemots were dead and quite a few of the others looked decidedly poorly. As long as an auk's eye is round it is doing well. Once its eye becomes oval that bird is in trouble. Eight guillemots looked hopeful that night, and so did the gannet, the shearwaters and the gull. Four more guillemots had by now arrived, covered in bitumen like the first ones, and they looked pretty seedy, too.

Tuesday was a superb day, and soon after breakfast Nona Rees arrived with a friend, an American girl called Bonnie.

They had come to help, they said, and had dressed for it. They certainly had – they were ready for anything, from arctic exploration to cleaning drains. They went off with Jean to feed and dose the birds while I kept records. This seemed a good opportunity to keep really careful records. We had enough guillemots for trends to be apparent and possibly statistically significant, but we didn't have so many birds as to make detailed recording too time-consuming or hopeless. I ringed each bird with a two-inch length of Dymo tape with a number on it, enough to go round the bird's leg three times, and I crimped the open end tight with pliers. These rings survived all the washing and swimming until the birds were properly ringed for release.

About mid-morning, we decided to try the toluene on the gull's tail and wing-tips, and we were getting ready when Ken Davies, a photographer from Carmarthen, turned up to film us for BBC TV. Jean and I had spoken on sound radio on quite a number of occasions but TV! Fame at last! He took a few shots in the treatment room and said he would film us cleaning the gull.

The fumes from the toluene were very strong so we used it out of doors, and Bonnie held a poncho with the bird's head through it to keep the fumes away. We lined ourselves up with the bird's head to wind, and I started applying the toluene. The bitumen came off almost at once and very soon it was obvious that it was all free of the plumage and just wanted removing. We could see that we could get it all off with successive washes with the solvent, but since all the remaining contaminant was now liquid, we decided to try washing it off instead. This would enormously reduce our consumption of solvent and we were much more sure of the result of washing with detergent.

It worked well in parts. The feathers soaked in solvent came up quite clean, but the bits at the end of the section well wetted with solvent still showed black and wouldn't come clean. We realized it was useless to try to use solvent only on the parts of a bird which actually had oil on. It was essential to treat the whole bird with it. Also, whatever else we had washed off, the smell of toluene remained. The fumes had been very strong and even in the open my head felt a bit swimmy because of it.

The bird, too, began to droop after a while, so we kept the poncho up to try to keep its head away from the fumes emanating from its tail. We played a fan on its head with the same object in view, but the poor thing died after about an hour. Then I found that though my hands were okay, my forearms had red blotches all over them. Right, I said, no more toluene.

While we were having a snack, it occurred to me that the hand cleanser we used in my depot, being a council purchase, must be the cheapest obtainable. I checked, and found out how much cheaper it was than the well-known commercial brands. It seemed probable that, being so cheap, it would not include the cosmetic ingredients which made the better known ones unsuitable, so I got hold of some to try. I sat on a stool, with a guillemot on a sheet of hardboard on my lap and a pot of cleanser handy, and with bated breath, I applied it to the bird while everyone else watched.

The hard crust of bitumen was soon softening at the edges. I carried on until I could be pretty sure that all the bitumen had been softened, and then washed the whole mess off with the usual detergent. In due course we had a beautifully clean bird. I went on sloshing hand cleansing jelly on more birds, Jean washed them, Bonnie rinsed them, and Nona buzzed round between us to pass things. We were in business, at last, and carried on till midnight.

We took time off to watch the early evening news, just in case we were on it, and sure enough we appeared on *Wales Today*. Ken Davies had taken a lot of film, of which only two minutes or so appeared, but we looked very professional, and the commentary was excellent. Ken had taken his indoor shots with a wide-angle lens so everything looked much bigger than it really was. We were delighted. One thing only was revealed to the watching millions, which I would have preferred to remain secret – there was a huge split in the seat of my ancient pair of jeans!

We started operations early the next day. Normally a bird is clean and just about dry in an hour and a half. Now we were faced with the better part of an hour for applying the hand cleanser, an hour for washing, so enormous was the mount of oil, and often much longer than usual to rinse. There was no way of being really sure that all the bitumen had been thoroughly softened and sometimes washing would show up a spot still resistant to the liquid. The hand cleanser would not act on wet feathers, so when this happened it was necessary either to dry the bird and start again, or give the offending spot a squirt of Co-op green from the bottle. This worked and was better for the bird but it gave rise to tremendous rinsing problems.

At midday, Margaret Patterson arrived with three more gillies, five shearwaters and two first-year gannets. The shearwaters were more in need of care and feeding than washing, though they had very slight touches of black on them, but the guillemots and the gannets were absolutely plastered like the earlier ones. One of the gannets had been named Mauritius, though we never found out why or by whom, and the other, which was stuffed in half a pair of jeans to stop it preening, we called Denim. Denim was a kindly, gentle creature for a gannet, but Mauritius was hell. Any approach was met with vicious stabs or scythe-like sweeps with an enormous bill. And he'd only been out of the egg for three months. We decided to have a go at washing a gannet, because if we could get Mauritius clean, we could clean anything.

It's normal to tape up an auk's bill before washing it, or to slip a tiny elastic band over it, but we don't like doing this with gannets because a gannet's nostrils are inside his bill. Once, very early on, we nearly suffocated a gannet by fixing his bill – he was visibly drooping before we realized what was happening, and his first few breaths when we released his bill sounded like a whale blowing. So with gannets, I usually hold the bird's head while someone else washes him. This means one hand loosely round the bill, the other behind the bird's head to stop him getting his bill free. The job is highly labour-intensive.

I sat on my stool, with Mauritius on my lap, while Jean held his head and Margaret stood by to pass things, and wondered how long it would take. His body was covered with bitumen one-eighth of an inch thick from his neck to his tail and there was quite a lot on his wings as well. To my delight, though it took much more hand-cleanser to clean a gannet than it did a guillemot, it didn't actually take much longer. After little more than an hour we were washing him. It took five washes before he looked presentable, but he came up splendidly under the shower.

Jean had held his head while I applied the hand cleanser and washed him, but as I carried him to the shower I held his head while she sprayed him. Right through these operations neither of us had taken the slightest chance with him. His cold eyes had been stolidly upon us all the time, and we were sure he was only waiting for an opportunity to have a go. We didn't give him one.

We washed Denim the same way. He was nothing like so aggressive, and under the shower he was so quiet, making no attempt to struggle, that I relaxed a bit. In a split second he had his head loose and gave Jean a slicing cut on her left cheek from the bridge of her nose to her ear. It missed her left eye by about a quarter of an inch. Never trust a gannet, never.

Both gannets were perfectly waterproof the next day, which was a big thrill, because the guillemots, though apparently spotless, were still wetting up in the tank. We were terribly concerned about their condition, too, because by the Thursday morning we'd had twenty-nine of them, but only twelve were still alive. Generally it is the lighter, more volatile, fractions of crude oil which are the most toxic, but the stuff on these birds had no light fractions in it. We were giving each one a daily dose of Milk of Magnesia, too, in the hope of counteracting whatever harm the oil had done to their insides.

The shearwaters were another problem. Their plumage is very soft and fluffy, and while it should have responded to washing like any other water bird we never actually tried it, and as there was so little oil on them we hoped we could get it off with fuller's earth. In fact it worked very well and all the shearwaters, bar one, which died, came up waterproof. On Thursday, the fifteenth, we were at it early again. Helpers, who of course had their own homes to run, didn't normally turn up until about 11.00. At about ten, Jean was in the bathroom rinsing a bird, I was on my stool inside the french windows of the bird room, daubing hand cleanser on a guillemot. Two strangers appeared outside the window, walking slowly past, apparently looking for someone to talk to. They didn't see me. After a while they came back again and I called to them but they obviously didn't know where my voice was coming from and they disappeared again. After a while they returned, and spotted me when I called out again. The window was shut, there was no way of opening it from outside, and, being covered in black oil to the elbows and having in my hands a bird even more lavishly covered and wanting only a second of release to flap its wings, I was in no state to open it. I told them to come in through the front door, which was open, like every door and window in the house, except the bird room one. I suppose they didn't like walking into a strange house with no one to greet them – I can understand their point – but obviously they couldn't understand why I didn't get up and let them in. They kept on passing the window, looking more and more indignant, and finally got to tapping on it each time they went by. Jean eventually came down and brought them in and they could see why I hadn't been able to move. Bless them, they were great. They were from the Midlands and stayed with us all day.

Their presence, along with our other helpers, gave me a chance to study my records and to see if any trends were in fact showing. One thing which everyone concerned with the treatment of oiled birds must do is to identify a symptom in a newly-arrived bird which will indicate that it is unlikely to survive. As long as the number of birds coming in is within a unit's capability this is perhaps not so important, but if the numbers are approaching saturation level it is very valuable to know which birds have the best chance so as to treat them first.

If a bird is going to die anyway, it might be better to give it an overdose rather than subject it to the trauma of handling it, and washing it, etc. Of the twenty-one guillemots we had taken in on Sunday, the first day, only eight were still alive. The rest had all died in the first three days, before we had washed them. Now I wanted to find a clear indication of a common factor in the birds that had died, a factor not present in the ones still alive.

I tried the amount of oil on the birds, which I had classified as slight, medium or bad – and the badly oiled ones were very bad indeed. Four of the survivors had been 'bad'. No indication there. I tried bodily condition on arrival. A healthy adult guillemot should weigh between two and two and a quarter pounds. Ours had weighed between 1 lb 4 oz and 1 lb 12 oz, though there was one of 1 lb 1 oz, a mere skeleton with feathers on. The survivors were all of different weights, spread between the two limits. Again no indication. Marks like those of a windscreen wiper on a bird's breast indicate preening, and a clean breast coupled with oiled flanks indicates a great deal of preening so, presumably, much ingesting of oil, too. To my surprise, the extent of preening seemed wholly unrelated to survival, and so did the amount of oil in the birds' droppings, also carefully recorded.

I had recorded the birds' food intake, by number of sprats per meal, and there I found the only significant trend. All birds have to be force-fed for a day or two after arrival, because they will not recognize dead fish on a plate as food. Most birds will take half a dozen or so sprats quite readily but sometimes a bird will refuse a fish and throw it across the room with a shake of its head. It is best then to give it liquid, plain water, perhaps, or better, Complan and glucose. All the survivors were birds which had never thrown a fish back, all the dead birds had refused fish on a few or many occasions.

This was no criterion for euthanasia, but it called for investigation so I belted off to the vet lab with a bag of dead birds, confidently expecting to find some indication high up in the gut of corrosion or irritation, caused by the oil, which would cause a bird to reject solid food. I hoped to find a suitable treatment, as well.

There was no such indication. There was no difference between the birds which had refused food often and those which had refused it occasionally – in fact there was no sign of damage to the gut of any bird at all. The cause of death appeared to be starvation. I well knew that many of the birds had been eating merrily after a day or so of refusal, but their insides were completely empty, like the others. I went home baffled.

Another guillemot had arrived while I had been out, and an adult gannet. The gannet, I was told, had a mind of his own, and washing him, and heaven knows he needed it, was an entertaining prospect. But wash him we did, on Friday, and he went into the outside pen with the others, dry as a bone. No more birds came in that day, and by the evening we could see light at the end of the tunnel. The gannets were fine, the shearwaters were fine, and the surviving guillemots, though not quite waterproof, were well on the way.

Saturday was a beautiful day, and we gave some of the gillies a second wash, reflecting in the intervals on the beauty of the birds in the sunshine. During the day we took in another gillie, a razorbill, a shearwater, another three gannets, and a heron. The heron was being chased across a field by a cow, we were told, and the cow was winning, so a spectator scooped him up and brought him to us. Malnutrition was his trouble, and a stone of sprats later he was a different bird, but the sea birds were all oiled like the earlier ones, and, the gannets apart, were desperately thin as well. We fed and dosed them and put them peacefully into their boxes, and in the evening went for a long walk on the beach.

On Sunday morning Peter Davies came to ring all the birds, and on Sunday afternoon we released the shearwaters. This needs to be done from a height, like a cliff top, because shearwaters have trouble taking off from a flat surface. Away went the birds, curving in a gentle westward arc, going home to Skomer. We went home and washed the three gannets.

All in all, we had had one herring gull, which had died,

nine gannets, eight of which were in the outside pen, perfectly waterproof and waiting for a fine day to be released, eight shearwaters, of which six had survived and been released, two razorbills, both of which were dead, and thirty-two guillemots, of which only eight were still alive, and weren't waterproof. Then, on Friday 23rd September, we had our first baby seal of the winter.

Tom Austin, the RSPCA Inspector for Pembrokeshire, brought her to Cardigan where we picked her up. She had a badly torn flipper, which had been lovingly and beautifully stitched by a vet in Haverfordwest, who had also given her the necessary injections, and with her came instructions as to when the stitches were to come out. We called her Bonnie after our American friend of only a week or so before, and gave her half a pint of Complan with a tube. She settled down in her box on a blanket and went to sleep. She was only three weeks old, because she still carried traces of her white coat, but she must have missed out badly on her post-natal feeding because she only weighed twenty-five pounds. This, coupled with her suspiciously gentle ways, made us very worried.

During the evening she passed a whole heap of black oil, including a lump the size of a tangerine. Obviously, she had been caught in the same oil as the birds but had moulted her white coat, and with it the external oil, before coming ashore. She hadn't been able to get rid of the oil inside her, though, at least not until she had her Complan. She died at 11.30 that night. The post mortem showed her gut clean of oil, but very badly eroded.

On the Sunday we took the gannets back to the sea. It's always a difficult job, releasing baby gannets, because they will almost certainly not have learned to fly and so will not know how to feed. Even so, we had given them a second chance and now it was up to them. We thought it would be nice to let them all go together, so we got bags of help and carried them, each one in its box, down to a secluded beach at New Quay. Six of them went off in style, but one baby and the adult stayed on the beach.

'We've got two things to worry about now,' I said to Jean, 'Nasty people who'll hurt them, and nice people who'll bring them back up to us,' and we went home for lunch. We went down at tea time to see how things were going, and the beach was empty. When we got home, though, there was Denim, faithfully brought back, as being apparently in need of care. We took him back again, and this time he went off merrily.

At tea time the next day, Jean got a phone call from some visitors to New Quay, asking about a big black bird which they couldn't identify and which had been on the harbour wall all day. It couldn't fly, they said, but they had been feeding it. A man had been fishing near them, and they had given it every fish he had caught. Their children had got the number from its ring, and, as instructed on it, had rung the British Museum, Natural History department, to tell them about it. The museum had been very civil but knew nothing about the bird, which was not surprising, since the museum is notified when a ringed bird is released, not when it is ringed. We went to collect the bird, and sure enough it was our old friend Denim.

We kept him for the day, then released him at dusk, which is probably the best time, but next day he was back on the harbour wall again. I took him to a much more secluded beach this time, and he not only swam away, after about fifty yards he took off and in a moment he was out of sight. We were much relieved on several counts, and gave hearty thanks that it was nice, peaceful Denim who had given all the trouble. The thought of children giving fish to Mauritius or trying to read his ring number kept us awake at night.

The following Saturday, 1st October, Tom Austin had another baby seal, and again we met him in Cardigan to pick it up. It was completely unmarked and very beautiful, but quiet and gentle. I knew by now what this could mean, and indeed, it died on the way home. The vet lab told us it was septicaemia. How on earth could a baby seal three weeks old be as infected as this one was?

We persevered with the guillemots, and all six survivors were clean and ready for release on 8th October. Off they went, diving and preening, as waterproof in the sea as they had been in our tank, but because they had been so difficult to rehabilitate and because we had been so worried at the possibility of having a seal wanting the tank at the same time, our reaction to their going was relief rather than joy. Even so, sincere relief is not an unpleasant emotion, and by supper time we were quite human again. By the time we went to bed we were quite convinced that, now we had no oiled birds, we would get no more seals either. We were wrong.

Two days later, Kevin Degenhard, the RSPCA Inspector from Carmarthen, brought us another seal, this time from Tresaith. It was the thinnest I had ever seen. It had moulted, so it would have been at least three weeks old, but it was so thin that I couldn't estimate its age beyond that. I could close my hands round it anywhere, and it only weighed twenty pounds. We christened it Winkle, having established it was a male, and took him to Aberaeron for Tom Herbert to give him his antibiotics. He was quite lively so we tried him first with some sprats, which went down, then with a smallish mackerel, which, with just the least bit of pressure, also went down. Eight mackerel later, we put him in his box, turned his lamp on, and he was asleep in a moment.

The next day he took a dozen mackerel, four each at breakfast, tea and bed time, and on each occasion he would have eaten more. Heaven knows he needed them but he was so obviously starved that we were afraid to give him too much at a time. He wasn't wheezing but he was breathing much too fast so we laced his fish with terramycin. He was terribly dirty so we popped him in the tank for long enough to scrub him a little. When we took him out he was shivering, so on went his lamp and all seemed to be well.

On the twelfth, Tom Austin brought another seal in, a white one this time called Pedro, nine or ten days old, weighing 38 lb. He was quite plump, though again much too quiet and peaceful, but his nose was hot so we rushed him over to Tom Herbert who gave him a massive dose of antibiotic. At nine o'clock he was dead. The post mortem revealed an abscess the size of a grapefruit inside him – in fact he was little more than bag of pus from midships to his tail. Again we wondered how any ten-day-old baby could be as bad as that. There was no external evidence of his abscess; if there had been, Tom would have operated to drain it. We sorrowed over Pedro, and persevered with Winkle.

At the end of the first week with us, Winkle started eating on his own, gently at first, but improving with practice, until after ten days he would swallow whole mackerel, herring and whiting – head-first normally, but if it was easier, tail-first. It was quantity he was after, not elegant manners. He couldn't go wrong, if he kept this up, and we thrilled at the thought of saving a pup as small as he had been. Very few people manage to save baby seals at all, and fewer still a twenty-pounder. After two weeks he was eating between twenty and thirty fish every day. All was not well, though, for he wasn't getting any bigger, and he wasn't putting on weight. We asked advice from everyone we could write to or telephone, and dosed him accordingly, but he stayed firmly at twenty pounds.

He died on 27th October, seventeen days after we had him, and he never stopped eating. Even so, his weight was still the same. All our previous seals had either died within a day or two as a result of conditions which were beyond treatment when they arrived, or had lived and been released. To lose a seal after nearly three weeks was a new experience and one we didn't like. I took poor Winkle to the lab, where they could find nothing wrong organically. He had starved to death, they said. I pointed out the amount he had been eating, and they showed me all the evidence of starvation – empty gut, no blood sugar, etc.

They did suggest, having regard to his very small size, that he might have been suffering from a syndrome which sometimes follows extreme exposure, that is starvation and acute hypothermia. It appears that if hypothermia goes far enough, and the sufferer has no food to metabolize, it will metabolize its own fat, but if this goes too far irreversible changes take place in its make-up and it will not again be able to assimilate food.

Winkle was obviously starving when he came to us, and, considering he would have had no blubber at all, low blood temperature was quite likely. We had fed him and warmed him straight away when he came in but evidently, by that time, it was too late.

This all seemed very odd and we followed it up, ending with correspondence with the Institute of Naval Medicine, whose Senior Medical Officer (Survival Medicine) said that the seal's symptoms were quite reasonable following extreme exposure. The same thing can happen to pigs, where it is known as the 'thin sow syndrome', and results from an inadequately fed sow trying to feed her litter in very cold weather. Once she has lost weight to a certain level, she will not be able to catch up, however much she is fed. The Naval doctor said that research in the whole matter would be very valuable and suggested we took the problem to our nearest medical or veterinary school, but as we haven't one anywhere near us, we haven't been able to pursue it.

The same thing can happen to birds, of course, and after much thought and consultation we feel pretty sure that that was the reason for twenty-six out of thirty-two guillemots dying while we were trying to clean them. They were oiled just after the breeding season, so they would have been underweight anyway, after the strain of feeding their youngsters in an area where their numbers put tremendous pressure on the fish stocks. And September is the time of their annual moult, which also takes it out of them. Several of them had had almost no flight feathers. They would have been on their way out to sea, and ample food, when they ran into the oil.

Also, they must have been oiled for quite some time before they came in, because while heavy fuel oil is a very viscous liquid, the stuff on them had passed the viscous stage – indeed, it must have hardened while it was on the birds. They had certainly been starving, since the pms had showed no body fat and very little muscle, and their history was such as to make hypothermia almost certain. We couldn't establish this, unfortunately, because we'd never taken their body temperatures. The gannets on the other hand had all been fat and healthy, bar one, which explains why we saved eight out of nine of them.

We had little chance to think too much about Winkle, because by the time we lost him we had taken over two more seals, neither of which was feeding itself at the time. The first was a fine, upstanding fellow of thirty-five pounds, with nothing wrong with him save that he knew nothing about eating fish. He arrived just as Winston Evans, the coxswain of the New Quay lifeboat, had brought us eight stone of whiting for Winkle. He had been supplying us all through the autumn, and we would have been lost without him, so we called this new arrival Winston on the spot. The second, which came in five days later, on the twenty-fourth, was as desperately thin as Winkle, and with many septic wounds. We named him Peter.

Winston had to be force-fed for nearly two weeks before he started eating on his own, but he made very little protest about it and the loss of blood on my part was minimal. He was big enough to be very hard to handle if the spirit had so moved him, so we wondered whether he was a more kindly specimen than some others we had met, or whether I was getting better at the act, for I was certainly able to feed him quite easily single-handed. He seemed to thrive right from the start. Winston the fisherman was very proud of his namesake, and Winston the seal had reason to be grateful to him: we got through a fantastic amount of fish that autumn and Winston supplied most of it. He had big plastic boxes with 'Winston, New Quay' on them, for his catches, and I tried hard to get a photograph of his namesake peering over the edge of one of the boxes, his head just over the legend.

Peter carried on just as Winkle had done. He ate prodigiously but never put on an ounce of weight. His wounds healed, his breath became sweet, and he got on very well with Winston, but our memory of Winkle was far too clear for us to be happy about him. I had to force myself to come and see him every morning, and each time I found him alive was a real relief. Winston was putting weight on so well that Peter showed up worse by comparison.

They were both still with us on 16th November, when Margaret Patterson brought us another infant of the breed, a white one, fat as butter, which we called Podger. He weighed sixty-five pounds, and had been lying on Newport beach for two whole days without moving. Even so, there was nothing obviously wrong with him and we merely gave him an anti-biotic injection and a half pint of glucose and Complan in case he was dehydrated. He accepted the tube with amazing gentle-ness, for all his size and energy, and while it was going down I found out why. His lower jaw was broken. Tom Herbert wasn't a bit worried about that. It would heal in no time, he said, just leave him alone. Happy that his odd behaviour was explained, we did as we were told, and crooned to him quietly to show we weren't just ignoring him. He was, of course, in the same room as Peter and Winston, and though Peter didn't move about much Winston used to lie alongside Podger's box and make little sighing sounds.

Two days later Podger was dead. Peritonitis, the vet lab diagnosed, following a perforated ulcer. How, we wondered yet again, did any two-week-old baby come to have a stomach ulcer, perforated or otherwise? How could we diagnose any-thing of the kind, let alone treat it after diagnosis?

The day after Podger had his post mortem, another baby seal arrived, five or six weeks old, quite plump, but very quiet. Jessie Ward and Bill Jones had found him on Cei Bach, and carried him nearly a mile along the beach. His quietness was understandable. He had lost his left eye, and the socket was obviously septic. His teeth were black, his mouth was black, and his breath was bad enough to take the paint off. Only a few days before, we had come across a piece of deathless poetry which ran –

> 'There was an old roadman called Kelly
> Who was complaining of pains in his belly.
> Said the doctor "It's gas,

With pills it will pass."
Now Kelly is well but he's smelly.'

So we called him Kelly.

Tom Herbert gave him far more antibiotics and ourselves far more instructions, than with any other seal we had had. When we got him home we tried to feed him, but he wouldn't accept a fish. I was not happy about force-feeding him, because sooner or later anyone who does it is going to get bitten, and whereas this normally results in nothing that Savlon won't fix, there are occasions when a little puncture wound becomes infected. Frankly I dreaded the possible outcome of a bite from Kelly's teeth. His mouth was in a really horrendous state, and I tackled the first feed with much circumspection. I got a few fish into him without much trouble, which was a great comfort. It was several days before I realized that his teeth were so bad he dared not bite me, it would probably have hurt him much more than it would me.

His eye socket was very bad for a week, then when I was feeding him one evening the abcess burst and a great gout of pus shot out. We were able to clean it out and pack it with antiseptic, and after another week the socket was perfectly clean. Seals appear to be able to live perfectly well with only one eye; indeed Stephen Evans keeps promising to show me a blind cow seal which has had her pups on the same beach for ten years. Kelly's mouth, though, wasn't improving, even though Tom Herbert called regularly, generally to give more antibiotics. Though the smell went, the teeth remained black and horrible. I gave Kelly ten or a dozen mackerel or whiting every day, and he seemed lively and quite happy. It also made a change to have a seal who seemed to love having his tummy scratched.

On 12th December, we took in our last baby seal of the winter. He was found in New Quay, and the only sign of trouble on him was a badly grazed nose. We called him Dylan. He resisted being fed in much the same way as Mo had done, which grieved me, because I had begun to feel a splendid confidence that it was my superior skill, not greater docility in the other seals, that had made feeding them so much easier. On the second day, though, he started eating on his own, and it seems likely that he was quite used to eating fish but didn't recognize dead ones as being food. It mattered little, because after five days he died. Dylan had a huge abcess inside him and he, too, actually died of peritonitis. Two days later, Kelly also died, of septicaemia as a result of his gingivitis.

Jean and I were very quiet for a couple of days after that. Kelly had seemed to enjoy shaking hands with us. He would grip one's hand with the little claws on his flipper, and would hold on for ages. Jean had actually been doing this with him when she felt his grip slacken and realized he was dying and that it was too late to do anything about it. We were almost afraid now even to look at Winston and Peter. Winston was enormous by this time, and spent much of his time alongside Peter as if to encourage him. Certainly Peter needed it. After two months and at least twenty stone of fish he wasn't a bit bigger. Or was he? As December went on, we began to think he *was* growing. By Christmas we were sure of it. He really was fatter. Somehow, he had overcome the 'thin sow syndrome' as it applied to seals, though it had taken ages, and it looked as if he would make it, with Winston. We thought of letting them go together.

By the middle of January, though, we decided that we had better release Winston. He was fat as butter, his coat was sleek, he was really fit, but he began to show the signs of restlessness we have come to associate with the wish to be away. There must be a way of keeping captive animals fit long-term or there would be no zoos, but it is an art we have not learned – and in fact do not wish to learn. All we want is to get our patients fit and back where they belong, and Winston duly went to Ceibwr on a lovely, crisp, calm day. Into the sea he went as if he'd only been out of it for half an hour, and we watched him from the headland as he turned west at the mouth of the bay and headed towards the haul-out.

Peter never looked back either, once Christmas was over,

and put on weight by leaps and bounds. We weren't taking any chances with him, in view of his medical history, so we fed him till he was even bigger and fatter and sleeker than Winston had been, and on 2nd March we took him to Ceibwr as well. Off he went, and, like Ripple, he was joined at the mouth of the bay by other yearlings. Peter went away with them in the right direction, and never came back. Nona Rees went to the beach night and morning for three days to make sure.

We reflected, as we went home, how lucky we were. To misquote the Good Book, there had been much more rejoicing over the two seals we had saved than sorrow over the seven we had lost. We didn't blame ourselves unduly over the seven. We had done all we could for them, we had enlisted all the professional help we wanted, it had always been freely and willingly given, and we had followed it. We did feel, though, that we could congratulate ourselves a little over Winston and Peter, particularly Peter. He had been so very sick, but he had gone off so well, apparently completely at home in what was, to him, an entirely new environment. Our delight at this was ample recompense for our strenuous efforts that autumn.

9

The Christos Bitas *Oiling*

One thing became crystal clear during the autumn and winter
of 1977. We simply had to have more room. For five weeks we
had looked after three seals, and for one week four seals, in the
bird room, but the experience was not something we cared to
repeat. All the fittings in the room are a foot off the floor to
make it easier to wash the place, but this gave wonderful hiding
places to our flippered friends. We blocked off most of the
space, but a determined seal can get past most things, and
Dylan, in particular, used to hinder our efforts by nipping at
passing ankles from his sanctuary under the sink unit. Any
room with seals in it has to be hosed down at least once a day
and the room just wasn't built for it. We were very lucky to
have only a few birds while the seals were with us. We needed
separate accomodation for seals and we took advantage of their
presence to finalize a design for a seal room.

It was going to cost at least a couple of thousand pounds,
without labour, and we could see no way of raising that locally,
in an area where the whole population inside a twenty-mile

11 A tricky job – getting hold of a baby gannet

12 One of our flippered friends ready for release

13 Lucy, the tawny owl, fully fledged

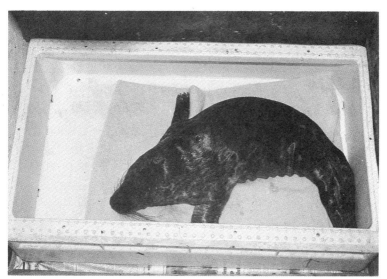

14 Peter on arrival, *p.131*

15 Peter, now looking much sleeker, ready for release, *p.135*

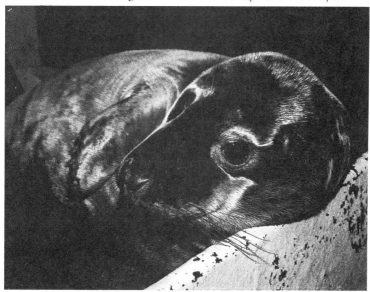

16 Henry and Bottle, the baby herons, *p.138*

17 Screwball, the gannet, *p.195*

18 Clean gannets in our outside pen

radius is only 30,000. Our financial situation needed improving by December 1977, so we remedied it by a coffee morning in Cardigan, under the banner 'Save our Seals'. Even so, we felt that consumer resistance was likely to become significant long before we had amassed £2,000, plus the routine money for food and so on, even if we could find the time to organize all the functions we would need. The last thing we could afford was to alienate the support we had always enjoyed by pushing it too hard, so we started to touch some of the trusts which made grants to suitably worthy causes.

We were prevented from brooding upon these problems by the arrival in early 1978 of a most unusual baby. Some men shooting wood pigeon near Llangoedmor found a baby heron on the ground, apparently fallen out of its nest. It had an injured wing, so maybe it had been pushed out. Anyway, they had watched it from a distance for most of the day but no parent bird came out to feed it so they brought it up to us. They began by protesting most energetically that they hadn't shot it, or its parents, but they need not have worried. We never quarrel with anyone who is shooting what he is entitled to shoot – far from it. We want people like that on our side. This quartet made it plain to us that they were as interested in saving the little heron as we were.

He did look most odd, a bundle of fluff with a huge bill sticking out of it. We unfolded him, very carefully, to make sure he really was all complete, for somewhere in the bundle were two wings and a pair of legs. It was a good thing, we felt, that there were mother herons about. Nothing else would ever love this chap. We bound up his wing and called him Henry.

Herons mostly eat fish, of course, but they also eat frogs, snails and slugs quite happily. In captivity they will even eat sausages with enthusiasm. Theirs is a high-protein diet, and they regurgitate partly digested food for their youngsters. We hadn't a clue how to simulate this, so Jean gave Henry bread soaked in Complan, together with mashed-up sprats and a little minced meat. Henry absorbed it all, in prodigious amounts, and impassively watched everything that was going on. By the end of the week we had revised our opinion of him. He still looked distinctly odd but he had totally endeared himself to us.

Then Peter Davies brought along another baby heron, this time from Tregaron Bog, just the same age as Henry and also with an injured wing. While Henry remained firmly folded up, this one was determinedly extended, looking like a half-gallon Strongbow flagon on stilts. We called him Bottle, accordingly, a more suitable name than Henry because there is no telling a male Heron from a female heron except by their behaviour and Bottle could have been male, or female or peculiar and still be suitably named. Actually we decided in the end that Henry should probably have been called Henrietta.

Both birds put on weight merrily and after a few weeks began eating whole sprats. Henry by this time condescended to show he had a pair of legs, but remained folded up on top of them. Bottle equally firmly kept his neck fully stretched. Quite soon we had to transfer them to an outside pen. We hadn't an indoor one with enough headroom for Bottle. We built them a nest of twigs, as nearly like the one their parents would have made as we could manage, save that it was only one foot off the ground, not fifty. Incidentally watching herons build their nests is an education. They do it before the leaves are on the trees, so it's quite easy to see them. Henry used to love being given a handful of twigs. He would add these to the nest until he was satisfied, and then systematically arrange them round Bottle's feet and legs. He placed them with great care and delicacy until he had a stack about six inches high and then Bottle, with a sort of a sigh, would slowly lift first one foot, then the other, and knock them all down. Henry would scream his head off for a minute or two then start again.

Although a heron is quite a big bird, it is very spindly, and is the one bird I am really unhappy to catch. I'm so afraid of hurting it. It's like catching a foor-foot spider. A heron, however, is a surprisingly sure flier. In the wild they fly in and out of their chosen tree, missing branches by inches but never actually touching them. Once, a heron flew from one end of our indoor tank to the other, a distance of six feet. He flapped his wings twice on the way and landed on a thin timber batten with perfect balance and rocked about no more than you or I would after taking a couple of paces forward onto a busy road. They were still with us in August, and though they were vastly entertaining, neither could fly. Each still had a damaged wing, and somehow neither was responding to treatment. Our fund-raising efforts had brought a good response, though, and on a memorable Saturday a JCB dug out the ground for the new seal unit. It was to be a building thirty feet by sixteen, with a store and treatment room at one end and a pool eighteen feet long, six feet wide and four deep in the other. There were to be six pens for seals which we might want to keep apart. We had a tractor-mounted concrete mixer and I started building. Laying bricks and working with concrete are things I know about, and though I was usually in the position of telling other people to do them, I have over the years developed a reasonable facility for doing them myself. Hence the no-labour charge in the estimates.

The normal autumn activity began on 2nd October when we had a phone message from Mrs Sutton, who lives right on the Teifi estuary, about a mile below Cardigan town, who feared for a baby seal lying on the tidal mud in front of her house. Jean and I went along. The seal had disappeared, but Mrs Sutton's son said he thought it was in the reeds the other side of an inlet and about a hundred yards away. The inlet was just mud at the time but would fill up to a depth of three feet or more at high tide, which was due in an hour and a half. We could see it creeping up the inlet but it had some way to go. A hundred yards straight across, half a mile at least round the end. Bryn Sutton and I were off like rockets, while Jean fetched the box to put the seal in.

He was a fine big fellow, five or six weeks old, and very cross with us for disturbing him. He was far too lively to carry – it would have been asking to be badly bitten – so the only thing to do was to pull him backwards by his tail. Seals don't like this much, but it's the only safe way to move one unless he's too ill to bite. The tide was very close by this time so off I went with the seal with Bryn in front to look for holes. After a bit he found one, but I went the wrong way, going backwards, and fell over in two feet of soft mud with the seal on top of me. He was less concerned with biting me than with escaping but I had to catch him again. It can't have taken that long to get him across the inlet but it seemed to be ages.

Tom Herbert gave him the usual injections and we took him home and fed him. That wasn't very difficult. Jean worked on him every day, tantalizing him with fish, and inside a week he was eating on his own. He was quite plump already and the weather was warm, so into the outside pen he went where he played in the water like a circus turn. When either of us went in with fish he would come humping up to us with the nearest approach to a smile of welcome I ever saw on a seal. He was lovely. On the Teifi we had found him so Teifi he should be.

Peter Davies came on Tuesday, the 10th, to ring all the birds we were likely to release in the near future and hoping to take Bottle back to release him where he had been found. But Bottle still couldn't fly, so he took with him another heron, an adult, which Kevin Degenhard had rescued from halfway up a sewer. The poor thing was glad to go. We had put it in with Henry and Bottle but neither of them would have anything to do with it.

On Thursday the 12th, the tanker *Christos Bitas* passed the wrong side of the Smalls light, hit the Hats and Barrels reef, and steamed all over the Irish sea, spilling oil all the way. This is it, we thought, this is the big one, just when we've got a seal that isn't anything like fat enough to release, and won't be for at least a month. We checked our stocks of everything and released six gulls which otherwise we might have kept for another week. We couldn't release Henry and Bottle, so we asked Peter Moss if he would take them, and they are in the Cardigan Wildlife Park still. We didn't want to see them go but we needed the space for the flood of birds that would surely come.

On the Monday the first birds arrived. This time there was

an effective organization to collect them. The West Wales Naturalist Trust office in Haverfordwest was open all day to co-ordinate collection and transport. Beaches had collection centres where birds were fed and dosed, put in ponchos, and kept warm and ready for transmission to a cleansing centre – either to us, or to the RSPCA centre at Little Creech, in Somerset. All the birds were poorly when we got them, so we changed their ponchos, fed and dosed them, and kept them quiet. They were all passing a lot of oil.

The next day, Tuesday, Ken Davies came up to make a film for BBC TV, and he made a beauty. A little of it appeared on the Welsh news that evening, which we saw, but most of it was shown on Nationwide the next night and we never knew it was on. It was even shown in Australia because I recently met a lady who had seen it there. Phil Davies, from Aberaeron, arrived to film for ITV also. All the while, more birds were being brought in, and on Wednesday, we started washing them, and very soon ran into trouble. Even after several washes, some birds still had a little black residue on them. However we rinsed our birds, they didn't come up as dry and fluffy as they should have done. In several cases we stopped rinsing before the job was finished because the birds were obviously beaten. Lots more birds arrived, and lots more people, but this time many of the people stayed to help – some of them with the birds, while others got meals and ran the Hoover round. One went away with all the laundry and returned with it beautifully pressed the next day. At five o'clock there was a change of shift. The adults went home and their place was taken by A-level schoolgirls who worked until ten or later.

Rinsing a bird takes much longer than washing it so to save time we installed a patent shower to work over the wash basin in the downstairs loo. Our Rayburn and immersion heater together are only enough to keep one shower going. Dave Crosswell, chairman of the local branch of the Trust, did the plumbing, and Hugh wired it up. That gave us two washing 'lines' which could be expected to push up output by 50%. During the afternoon Meurig Jenkins arrived to record a spot for Good Morning Wales on BBC Wales Radio 4 the next morning. He suggested that if we wanted to appeal for something now was our chance. I asked for old flannelette sheets to make ponchos, and old towels for the birds to stand on. Little Creech keeps its birds on floors with half an inch of water on them, but we prefer wet towels, to keep their feet soft.

Early in the evening, David Saunders rang to ask if we would take an oiled baby seal and look after it. Being full up, as I saw things, I wondered if he could find someone else to take it. No, he said, he couldn't. He could send more birds to Little Creech and fewer to us, but no one else could handle the seal, and he told me how it had been picked up. When crude oil emulsifies naturally under wave action in a choppy sea, it forms a brown blanket looking like chocolate mousse. A huge mass of this had drifted into the north haven on Skomer and Stephen Evans of the Nature Conservancy had had to watch helplessly while baby seals tried to pass it to get to the beach. They couldn't rise through it to breathe and, frantic to get their noses out of the stuff, they were sinking for good. Stephen had managed to get hold of one, which he was now asking us to take. He would bring it up later in the evening. I thought of the effort Stephen must have made to get hold of it, to get it to the mainland, and of the sixty miles extra motoring he faced. I thought of a baby seal with its mouth, its nose, its ears and its eyes full of corrosive oil. Particularly I thought of its eyes. I couldn't refuse.

Stephen arrived at about 11.30, and he had with him his father, a retired vet, John Davies, sometime warden of Skomer, and another colleague. We examined the baby, which was absolutely soaked in oil, and found that its eyes did not in fact appear to be harmed. Much encouraged, we decided to get the worst of the oil off straight away and got down to it with Co-op green and a hosepipe. Unlike a bird, a good scrub will not hurt a seal, and though he didn't like it one bit we got an enormous amount of oil off him without bloodshed. We rinsed his eyes with particular care until he didn't blink any more than normal and we judged we had all the oil away from them. The baby was still in his white coat, less than three weeks old, so a milk diet was called for, and I duly slipped a tube down his throat and Jean and Stephen's father between them pumped in half a pint of glucose and Complan, laced with dianimol to help him pass any oil he had ingested and with Milk of Magnesia to counteract its effects.

I was tremendously glad I was able to do this with some facility and confidence. Without something inside him that seal was doomed, and apart from our obvious obligation to the seal we owed something to the quartet which had gone to so much trouble on his behalf. They all knew much more about seal behaviour than we did, except that they didn't know how to handle and treat a sick one. They were very appreciative and when they'd gone, and the seal, now called Skomer, had bedded down, we went to bed feeling a bit uplifted. We slept like logs, or at least I did, until, at 5.30 am Jean woke me. 'Skomer's loose,' she said, 'He's outside somewhere.'

While I was fitting my slippers the milkman drove in. About three seconds later he drove out again. To his credit, the bottles were in their usual place and unbroken but what he must have thought we can only imagine. The sight of something like a four-foot brown-and-white slug, travelling rapidly up the drive at half-past five in the morning, is not a thing to be taken lightly.

How Skomer ever got the window open remains a mystery, and we hauled him back with much relief. Thank goodness Jean had heard him. Where he would have got otherwise makes the mind boggle. We gave him another feed, as a result of which my sheepskin slippers still bear traces of the oil on his tail, and bedded him down again. We got dressed then, and put the radio on to try and hear ourselves. Our bit came on about 7.15 am and lasted two-and-a-half minutes. The appeal was there, unabridged and unedited we were glad to note, so we said, ah well, we'll see what happens, and started washing guillemots.

At 11 am, a man drove up in a Ford Granada estate, full to the back with towels and sheets from Llanelli. In the afternoon a lady arrived in a Vauxhall estate the same size, full of towels and sheets from Milford Haven. The next day Ivor and Elaine Evans came from Hereford with a Dormobile full up with the same items. Dozens of local people brought us stuff, too. The appeal had worked superbly, and many of the towels were better than the ones we have in our bathroom.

During the morning, over coffee, we had a contemplative look at Skomer. We hadn't room for him in the bird room but he was quite fat enough to be outside. He was still quite oily in patches, though this would not hurt him because when he moulted, within a couple of days, all the oil would come off with his white fur. Even so, we decided to give him another wash to enhance his self respect, then put him in the outside pool, with Teifi. Skomer promptly decided that Teifi was his mother and chased him all over the pen until Teifi did some alarming rock climbing to get away.

This episode had only just finished when two characters arrived with a car full of exceedingly expensive kit and announced that they were from ITV's News at Ten. Somehow they had heard that we had an oiled baby seal, and wanted to film us washing it. I said I was sorry but we'd just washed it, and I led them to see it. It was still oily, they said. Couldn't we wash it again? I said that the poor thing had had enough for one day. They pointed out their, and my, 'duty' to the public to give it interesting things to view. I pointed out my duty to the seal. There the matter would have rested, only it occurred to me that it was time Skomer was fed again, so they decided to film us doing that instead.

Now it is essential to keep the seal's mouth open while the tube is in his throat, or he will bite through it in a flash and swallow it. I keep my left thumb, or at least the basal joint of it, in the seal's mouth for this purpose and wear two foundry men's gloves on that hand while I do it. A seal's teeth won't reach the skin through them, though he can bite hard enough to hurt. When that happens I derive no end of relief by expressing my opinions in terms which would evoke at least mild disapproval from the Vicar and would no doubt have to be replaced on the air by little whistles. Jean is well used to my language, and sympathizes. This time, however, I found the presence of three feet of sausage microphone pointed at me most inhibiting. Instead of a short burst of Anglo-Saxon, the best I could manage was something like 'Ooooh . . . he's . . . biting me!' Very unsatisfactory, and no relief at all, and not helped by Jean, who was beside herself with laughter as she pumped in the Complan.

The two photographers wandered around for a while and then disappeared. We never appeared on News at Ten. Anyway, they didn't bother us after filming us feeding Skomer so we got down to some serious bird washing. We had plenty to do. By tea-time that Thursday we had received seventy-four birds, all guillemots and razorbills, quite a number of which had perked up enough to be ready for treatment. I soon began to appreciate what is meant by 'slaving at the kitchen sink'. I was slaving at the bird room sink, not the kitchen one, but by half past ten I had tried standing on a plank of timber, standing the bowl on a plank in the sink, perching by back-side on a stool, anything to change the angle of my back. From Friday tea time, the girls took over from the adults. The coming week was half-term, and they were going to help us whatever happened. Kirsty and Ceridwen Young, Helen Flawn and Alison Rees hardly left the place. They would be with us by eight in the morning and didn't leave until late evening. They received each bird as it came in, started its record, fed and dosed it. They did all the feeding and recording of the birds, and a lot of the rinsing. On Saturday Stephen Jaremko, who has done the illustrations for this book, turned up, announced that he was going to stay for the week in our caravan, and settled in. After everyone else had gone to bed, Stephen used to creep into the bird room to sketch the birds.

Saturday brought one family of four who sat in our living room all day making ponchos. I have an idea they got lunch, too, but no one could be sure afterwards. It also brought Tim Stowe, the biologist of the RSPB, and Peter Hope-Jones of the National Museum, in Cardiff. They were researching into ageing in guillemots, for which they wanted all the dead ones. They took them from the freezer, twenty-seven of them. That left us with fifty-seven, most of which had been washed and looked fine, but they weren't quite waterproof even after, in some cases, a second wash. They might have been happier out of doors, since the weather was perfect, but of course Teifi and Skomer were in the outside pen. Hugh and two of his friends ran up a temporary pen on the site of the future seal pool, with a children's paddling pool in it. But the birds showed no enthusiasm for it. The seals might well have liked it, but they'd have wrecked it in half an hour. Heavens, how we wished the seal unit was working.

More worrying still that Saturday, Skomer went off his food, and brought up a nasty mess looking like curdled milk. Tom Herbert gave us some recommendations but the same thing happened at tea-time and again at supper. Also, quite suddenly, he had become very lethargic. On Sunday morning he was no better, and we wondered whether we should start weaning him off milk. He was just about to moult, so he would have reached the end of his mother's feeding in the wild, but we couldn't imagine that was a valid reason for refusing and regurgitating anything so harmless as Complan and glucose. On Sunday afternoon we had a message about a white baby seal on the harbour wall in New Quay so Hugh and I went to collect it. It was the smallest pup we had ever seen, and half an hour after bedding it down it died. Half an hour later Skomer died, too. I took them both to the vet lab, where they told me that the New Quay pup had almost certainly never had any food in its life, and that its organs had long passed all hope of redemption. Skomer's inside, I was also reliably informed, was very badly eroded, and he had kidney and liver trouble as well, all no doubt as a result of the oil.

We spoke of the captain of the *Christos Bitas* in terms which would have provoked a breach of the peace. He had steamed the wrong side of a lighthouse, holed his ship and refused to stop. The result was there in my lap, and all around me, and I wanted him to see what he'd done. It's as well he didn't, because I would never have kept my hands off him. Killing a few thousand birds and seals is evidently not an indictable offence, but I would have ended up in jail.

One thing we had to be thankful for, *Christos Bitas* had been pumped out and sunk, so her capacity for mass desecration was over. The oil which had escaped had all been sprayed and dispersed, or, where it had come ashore, been picked up.

This use of dispersant began to worry us. We had had plenty of birds before which had been difficult to get properly waterproof but we had never had quite the trouble we were getting now. The birds were so nearly waterproof, but not quite right. They would come up perfectly after rinsing, as dry as anyone could wish. They would float high in the water, apparently perfect, but after fifteen or thirty minutes they would begin to wet up. We couldn't possibly release them, but we dreaded keeping them, because of all the ills which befall them in unnatural surroundings. We persevered all the week, washing the fittest birds again. There were some behavioural characteristics, too, which were strange. Had the birds got dispersant on them, and in them, as well as crude? It was the only new ingredient we could think of, but there was no way we could find out. We sent half-a-dozen bodies to the vet lab, after taking all the measurements that Peter Hope-Jones wanted, and though they found nothing to help us get them waterproof, they isolated salmonella in nearly all of them. You can imagine how our recourse to soap and water, always high on these occasions, increased dramatically.

We took a night off, the Friday of the second week. Living not far away is a man who works as a chef on one of the cruise liners, and occasionally, when he's home, he cooks a magnificent curry supper in the pub in the village. You can have your own curry hot, very hot or explosive. One of these memorable occasions was that Friday, so off we went, family, adult helpers, teenage helpers, indeed everyone who had helped us. We had a grand evening and it did us a power of good.

Then during the weekend, we took a careful view of the position. We had rather been looking at trees than the wood, and perhaps a night away made all the difference. We had had 118 birds by that time of which 67 were still alive, nearly all washed, some of them several times, but not one was truly waterproof. I rang John Hughes at Little Creech to see how he was faring. He was having trouble, too, but he had got some birds waterproof by particularly thorough washing and rinsing. Yes, he was using Co-op green as well, nothing else. He had no idea what was on the birds to make them so hard to clean, but agreed that this was the most difficult bunch he'd met. Even so, some birds, particularly those he or his wife had washed personally, were ready for release.

If he could do it, so could we. We selected the fattest and apparently fittest guillemot and washed it carefully yet again. We examined it with a powerful glass for traces of residual oil at the base of the feathers, but could find none. We rinsed the bird for well over an hour, taking it in turns to make sure we'd missed nothing, and it was clean and dry and fluffy. The water from the shower was pearling off it as if it was made of polythene. We left it overnight to rest, and the next day put it in the tank, extra specially scrubbed for the occasion. For twenty minutes it floated high in the water, splashing the water all over itself vigorously – doing all the right things, but then it began, very slowly, to sink. We tried other birds, but every one remained, obstinately, just a little bit short of waterproof. I was at a loss as to what to do next.

I rang Tim Stone at the RSPB to see if he could help, but he couldn't. Nor could Dr Croxall, now part of the British Antarctic expedition, whom I managed to locate in Cambridge. I was sure that there was something on these birds which we hadn't met before. If so, it must be of hydrocarbon origin, part of the original crude; if so, some kind of hydrocarbon solvent should get it off. I tried the hand cleanser which had worked so well on the gannets the year before, but that had shown its effectiveness on heavy oil which had not really penetrated the plumage. This, whatever it was, must reach all the way to the skin, and the hand cleanser, being a jelly, couldn't follow it without an unacceptable amount of feather disturbance.

The awful thing was that all the time birds were dying, one or two every day. Some died as a result of the oil itself. Even if the bird survived the action of acidic oil on its digestive organs, its liver and kidneys were quite likely to be fatally affected. Some birds undoubtedly suffered from the starvation-hypothermia syndrome which had killed Winkle. Hardly any of our birds was putting on weight. Then there was the salmonella.

Little Teifi, however, was a great consolation during all this. He was putting on weight steadily and by the beginning of November we were thinking of releasing him. We needed the pen he occupied in solitary state or we would have kept him just as a consolation, as evidence that we could do something right. There had never been anything wrong with him except that he had not learned to eat fish and, being on his own, never would. He had been relatively easy to feed, and had never been aggressive. I used to go into his pen and tell him about our troubles with the birds and he would listen attentively with his head on my foot. All I ever had to show from our conversations was a wet shoe, but they always did me a power of good.

We took him to Ceibwr on 7th November, and off he went, like all the others, as if he'd only been on the beach for a nap. He swam out of the bay, in due course, turned west as we wanted him to do, and disappeared. It was wonderful to see him go, and that feeling of elation at having saved a very beautiful and, for a time, helpless animal was again strong upon us as we watched him. It would have been nice to have been releasing Skomer as well, though.

At least Teifi's release gave us an outside pen back, and we put the best of the surviving birds in it in the same day. They had become reluctant to go into water, which is a bad thing, because unless they swim regularly they will not preen and unless they preen their waterproof properties will be lost. Again, their 'false knee' joints tend to develop an arthritic infection with leaves them stiff and useless unless they are much in the water. They were much more enthusiastic in the proper pen, diving and preening, but they still tended to be wet so we gave them an infra-red lamp at night.

They seemed quite happy in the outside pen for about a week, going into the water on their own and preening merrily afterwards. They didn't become properly waterpoof, though, and after that first week they stopped going into the water at all. So we brought them back indoors again, where it wouldn't be quite so cold for them. They began swimming once more. Every day, though, another bird or two would lose condition and in spite of all our best efforts it would die. More oiled birds kept coming in, twos and threes at a time, from all over the coast, and these were treated, too. Whether they had the same stuff on them as the first *Christos* birds we didn't know. It's generally believed that once there has been a big oiling every cowboy tanker skipper washes his tanks into the sea for weeks, knowing very well that no one can establish who is responsible, so these birds could have been oiled almost anywhere. 10th November was a particularly bad day – five birds died.

On Saturday the 11th, all the New Quay Scouts came up to do a sponsored work-in for us. Two boys were really interested in the birds, so Jean let them wash and rinse one, which they did perfectly. Others gave the bird room the scrub-up of the year. We pulled down the temporary pen Hugh had built, and concreted some of the seal building floor. That was a valuable bit of therapy for me. I was beginning to think that the world consisted solely of not-quite-waterproof auks and pens for them to live in. The Scouts were great, and three weeks later they gave us all the sponsorship money, too, £50 of it.

On Sunday, 19th November, we took charge of yet another seal. This one had been found by some skin divers at Martins Haven, trying to climb out of the surf onto some rocks and getting badly knocked about in the process. When they managed to get hold of it, they found it was covered in oil. It looked just the same as Skomer had looked, and we dreaded the implications. We found that it had moulted, so we made a through job of the cleaning because this one would not be losing its oil in the process of moulting. He was a fine, fat fellow, and didn't much object to being given a mackerel or three. Very probably he was used to fish, but not used to finding dead ones lying about. The divers had called him Flipper so we did, too. Flipper's droppings were normal, no oil in them, and he hadn't been dehydrated, so the prognosis was bright. In a couple of days he began eating on his own and we stopped worrying about him.

The birds were still bothering us, though. Jean washed a couple every day during November, and many evenings we would both wash a couple more. Some of them must have been washed a dozen times, always with the same result, beautifully dry after showering, wetting up after half an hour in the tank next day. The same process went on in December. Try as I would I couldn't find anyone who could help. I learnt that the *Christos Bitas* oil had been a light Iranian crude, which was particularly toxic, but no one could tell me why we couldn't wash it off or, perhaps, what part of it we couldn't wash off. The residue after evaporation of the lighter fractions should be bitumen, and bitumen is black. There was none on any of our birds.

We took Flipper back to sea on 21st December, fit and fat, and by the New Year we had only one *Christos Bitas* bird left, whom we called, predictably, Solo. He died in February, and the *Christos Bitas* incident was over. It would be nice to add 'bar the shouting', but there was no shouting. A year after the incident an inquiry, held in Greece, found that the captain's errors and omissions amounted to gross negligence, but no disciplinary action was ever taken.

10

The Ignorance of Man

Behaviour is thinly covered in books about wildlife, and while I can understand why this should be, I look forward to the day when the situation will change. An immense amount of observation is necessary before any safe conclusions can be reached on the meaning of a particular action of, say, a bird, and behaviour is terribly difficult to describe, anyway. Birds cleaned of oil and introduced to fresh water have a most distinctive behaviour pattern when they are waterproof or nearly enough so, something I have seen many times. But to describe the bird's actions unequivocally so that someone else could be completely sure that his bird was waterproof would be beyond me.

Maybe we will have to rely on the visual arts rather than the written word for our education in behaviour but a film or a television show is a transitory thing and once seen is generally gone for good. Until video recorders become as common as portable radios, few of us will be able to pull a television show off a shelf like a book, to check on something in it. Anyone, the first time he sees a bird in the wild that he has just seen on film, would want to see the film again. Perhaps, one day, we will have books illustrated with video tape. Read a few pages on how a heron catches fish then turn the set on for a demonstration.

The real-life counterparts of Tom Forest of 'The Archers' are treasures to the earnest student of wildlife behaviour. They have actually been watching it all their lives, can interpret it and recount it. They know whose barn has an owl in it, whose tree has a buzzard's nest, when the baby swallows are ready to fly. They know a warning cry from a love call, know what bird made it, and will soon show you why. 'When a barn owl sways about like that he's warning you off. It's a threat posture. You've invaded his patch.' Some of this breed appear on television and I hope there will be many more. We had one chap living near, and an hour with him was worth a month in a library. He was most amused, once, to hear that someone had been given a grant to study some aspect of a particular bird's behaviour. 'I could have told 'em that for nothing,' he said, and I'm sure he could, but no one knew it except himself. He was always going to start writing but he never did – very few of his type ever do. They much prefer watching and showing their friends what's new, and they don't seem to realize the wider value of what they have picked up over the years.

In comparatively recent years, though, the observation and codification of wildlife behaviour has become a respectable field of investigation and there has emerged a new breed of expert with the powers of observation of a game keeper and the scientific approach of a professor. More and more such people are emerging, following the lead of Konrad Lorenz, and a splendid example is the late Prof. H. R. Hewer, whose book *British Seals* is compulsive reading to anyone interested. Therein you may read not only about the astonishingly large size of certain of the grey seal's blood vessels and how, unlike the dolphin, it exhales before diving, but also much about its behavioural characteristics. To get his information, Professor Hewer spent many years peering from the top of some of the most inhospitable cliffs in Britain, during the nastiest months of the year.

Unlike Hewer, many people rush into print without doing their homework. He quotes a work published in 1936 as containing twenty-seven firm statements on seal biology, of which twenty-two were wrong. I read, not long ago, a firm statement that seals feed by eating fish, swallowed whole, head first, and in no other way. But not one of our seals has failed, at some time or another, to tear its fish to bits before swallowing it, and as for invariably swallowing fish head-first I've seen fish swallowed tail-first many times and, once or twice, doubled up. The big bull seal on the Llanina reef would bite selected pieces from his mullet and discard the rest. A book about seals or, more specifically, about the culling of them in the Orkneys, published in 1979, states that seals use their tail flippers for close manoeuvering and their front ones for going places. An interesting observation – but he'd got it the wrong way round.

Almost every reference to puffins will quote the fact that they somehow catch a fair number of fish in their beaks, always holding them crosswise, which must save them an awful lot of effort in feeding their youngsters. A puffin has the usual pair of backward-facing hooks on its tongue, and the inner face of its upper mandible, the roof of its mouth, is a bit like a cheese grater, but nowhere can I find an account of just how he uses those features to hold a number of fish at one time. Or why razorbills and guillemots, which have the same general equipment, only take their fish one at a time.

My own experience gives me a great sympathy for the earnest observer in this field. I've probably had a better chance of watching guillemots feeding than most people. Once they are clean and waterproof we try to build them up to their proper weight before releasing them. They stand in little groups, and from time to time one of them will decide to eat a fish. It paddles over to the dish, where it is soon joined by others, and they all stand like a lot of little men in tails round a circular bar. A bird will pick up a fish and, after due consideration, turn it from the initial crosswise position and swallow it head-first. This is a positive and fully controlled action, though it's done in a flash, and while I've watched it hundreds of times I can't work out any feasible sequence of bill and tongue movements to explain it. If I can't explain how a guillemot turns a fish in its bill, something I can watch from two feet away at almost any time, I have to admit that explaining the puffin's multi-fish capability, practised under water and some way offshore, presents difficulties.

A knowledge of what is normal behaviour in a bird is of enormous value to anyone trying to treat a sick one. A fit guillemot stands upright and its eyes are bright and round, a sick one tends to lie down and its eyes tend to an oval shape. When a guillemot stands on the webs of its feet with its 'heels' well up, it is getting on really well. But there are dozens of other regular guillemot characteristics which may or may not be significant, and the Oiled Seabird Research Unit at Newcastle recognized this and did a lot of research into guillemot behaviour. Unfortunately, though they reported their observations in some detail, they never published any conclusions. Over the whole subject lies the snag that what a healthy bird does in the wild may bear little relation to what it will do in a cage or a pen. Sick birds sit, immobile and impassive, indicating that something is wrong but giving no indication what it is.

A bird's droppings can be very informative as to its condition, but one needs to know what the bird's normal droppings should look like. To examine the 'normal' droppings of a guillemot is far from easy because the cliff ledges on which they breed, the only place on shore where they can be seen at all, are hideously inaccessible and inches deep in droppings anyway. It's obviously desirable to stop dosing a bird to help it pass oil when it has no more oil to pass, something shown by the return of its droppings to 'normal'. Jean and I spend a lot of time studying nasty little blobs on pieces of paper to decide whether they are normal or not. If only advice was available which makes it crystal clear what is meant by droppings that are 'normal.' It takes me back to my army days, when they used to tell us, in Burma, that if we ran out of proper rations it was quite safe to eat anything a monkey ate. The advice would have been more valuable if they had also told us how to get close enough to a monkey to see what it was eating or told us just what a monkey did eat.

The situation is quite different where birds of prey are concerned. The raptors have been studied in the greatest detail for centuries, in captivity as well as in the wild, in the course of falconry, and the Hawk Trust exists to serve the people who have a love of raptors – and the birds themselves. Its members have their idiosyncrasies – a falcon doesn't have droppings, it has 'mutes' – and there is no such thing as a beak in their conversation, it's always a bill. We have several very keen members living near, and they are always ready to help us with sick birds of prey. It can take a great deal of time and patience to re-introduce to the wild a bird which has been in captivity for a long time, with an injured wing, say, but the hawk people are always happy to do it for us. They call the process 'hacking' the bird back. It used to be great to have a knowledgeable hawk man with us wardening the peregrines. 'It's quite normal for the tiercel to have a regular perching rock a hundred feet or so away from the eyrie,' one of them told us, 'and when he brings prey in he'll take it to his perch and stay there for a time while the falcon calls to him, before he actually delivers it to the eyrie.' It was nice to know. It had seemed very wrong to us.

Our knowledge of the other species may be centuries behind our knowledge of raptors, but we are catching up. I have wondered for years how an oystercatcher manages to open shellfish to get at the inside. Oystercatchers eat all kinds of shellfish except oysters but are particularly fond of mussels. No human can open a mussel without using a knife or crushing the shell, and the oystercatcher's bill, which is long and slender, seems hopelessly weak for the job. I found the answer in a delightful book by Hugh Falkus, called *Nature Detective*. They do it by 'stabbing' or 'hammering'.

A stabber looks for mussels in shallow water with their shells slightly open to admit the plankton they live on – the normal condition of a mussel under water – and thrusts its bill into the gap at just the right angle to reach the adductor muscle which holds the halves of the shell together. It cuts this with the tip of its bill, after which it can do what it likes with the mussel.

A hammerer selects a mussel in the dry, prizes it off its rock and, using its bill like a pickaxe, punches a hole in the shell near the adductor, then cuts the muscle through the hole. It levers the shell open, cuts and scoops the flesh into a single blob and eats it. A well-practised oystercatcher, say four years old, can do this in about thirty seconds.

Once a stabber always a stabber, once a hammerer always a hammerer, and no stabber ever hammers or vice versa. Each teaches its young its own technique, something quite fascinating to me. But we have a fledgling oystercatcher ready for release in all ways, save that we can't teach it to open shellfish. If anything, finding out at last how an adult bird does it has made the teaching even more difficult. We can only release him near a flock of his brethren – that's easy enough – and hope that he learns from someone.

The homing ability of pigeons is well enough known if inadequately explained, but we seem to have found an extension to it which deserves thought. There are dozens of doves and pigeons at Penfoel – some living in proper cotes but most perching all over the house, to the ruin of the roof gutters and the window-sills – which are often joined, particularly at feeding times, by large numbers of homers whose route in a race passes nearby. Some of these are hurt, and the injured ones behave quite differently from the fit ones. They will sit on the front doorstep or the step of the french window of the treatment room. If that window is open they will go inside and wait on the worktop. They wait to be picked up and are quite happy to be handled. Once, Jean was weeding among the roses by the front door when a strange pigeon came up and stayed close to her hand. After a while she noticed that it had a broken leg and an injured eye. Fit birds would never approach a person so boldly, but so many injured ones have that we have no doubt they are quite deliberately seeking treatment. But how do they know that it is available or where to come? Is there a far more sophisticated method of communication between birds than has been suspected?

A summer or two ago, my daughter, Diana, found a couple of baby magpies on the ground and a dead adult magpie, not far from a wrecked magpie's nest. No other adult had appeared in an hour, so she decided to bring the babies in for Jean to look after them. This was on a Sunday morning, and when we got back from church at about half-past three there was another baby magpie on the doorstep, exactly the same size as the other two. It made no attempt to get away but tamely accepted being handled and when it was put with the others there was every evidence of happy reunion. We have no real doubt that it was related to the two Diana had found, but how had it made its way over a quarter of a mile of ground it had never seen, to join its siblings? It was far too young to fly.

Further research is certainly called for in the treatment of oiled birds. The Newcastle method is very effective on most birds and with most crudes, but we find all too often that birds are contaminated with something which doesn't respond, or not fully, to washing-up liquid. This is the only cleansing agent recommended, so when it fails we are on our own. The heavy fuel oil of 1977 had been a perfect example of this, but we had found that the hand cleanser of Applied Chemicals, Ltd, would soften it enough to make it respond to the normal washing process. But like most hand cleansers the product is a gel, and it won't follow dried-up crude right through a bird's plumage without disturbing the feathers so much that the bird would never restore them however much it preened. A light oil is the answer here, but finding something suitable is far from easy. Most commercial oils embody additives which may themselves be impossible to wash off.

The *Christos Bitas* birds had been another case. We got them very nearly dry, but not quite, so we couldn't release them. The contaminant was very light, and the lighter oils are the more toxic, and the poor birds died one by one before we could manage to shift the last half per cent of whatever was on them. Much of the Irish sea had been sprayed with chemicals to disperse the oil, and we wondered whether this was the cause of the trouble. The chemical used, BP1100 X, is an emulsifier, the same kind of thing used to clean parts of motor engines. It gets the oil off, but, being highly surface active, leaves a very thin film, just one molecule thick, on anything it comes into contact with. A chemical designed to emulsify oil wouldn't dissolve in oil or it wouldn't emulsify it, and it wouldn't dissolve in water or it wouldn't emulsify anything. While the film would be wholly undetectable, it would be enough to keep the bird waterlogged, and extremely difficult to wash off. No problem on a piston, but disaster on a bird. But we'd had birds with the naturally emulsified oil, the chocolate mousse, on them, and they had been just as intractable, so we had to look further for our villain.

I think we found it, in the end, quite by chance. At a seminar on cleaning oil-polluted beaches, something I was professionally concerned with, I was given a pamphlet on BP1100 X, and on the back page was a schedule of the oils imported into this country, giving the physical properties of the oil and its port of origin. Light Iranian, the *Christos'* cargo, was listed under 'Medium wax content', so what we couldn't shift was probably a very small amount of wax, deposited, perhaps only in patches, as the lighter fractions of the crude evaporated. Unlike the bitumen, which would have been similarly deposited but which we could see and which we finally got off, the wax would have been undetectable. The answer to this, and to residual bitumen, is to soak the bird in a light oil, which will soften the contaminant and make it respond to household detergent. We now have two samples of oil from BP and some odourless kerosene from Esso to do the job so we now feel more confident, but we found all this out far too late to save the *Christos* birds.

If there are gaps in our knowledge of how to clean oiled birds, there are chasms in our knowledge of the best medical treatment for them. This is just as important, because there is little virtue in having a beautifully clean, dry bird if it promptly dies from some illness induced by the oil or from being in

captivity. The Newcastle recommendations of 1972 had something to say on the subject, but Dr Croxall, who did much of the
Newcastle research, wrote a chapter on oiled birds in a book
called *First Aid and Care of Wild Birds*, published in 1978, and
says rather less in it than he said in 1972. The International Bird
Rescue Research Center, of Berkeley, California, has published
an excellent booklet on treating oiled birds, but it makes no
recommendation on medication. It merely says much more
research is required. Little Creech, the Mousehole oiled bird
centre in Cornwall, and ourselves, all give different initial doses
to our birds. None of us is doing anything actually wrong, but
one of the three treatments must be best, and if someone would
tell us which it is, we would use it.

So there is a vast field for research in the behaviour of wild
birds and animals, both sick and healthy. There is an immense
amount of information already available but locked in papers to
learned societies and in the minds of keen observers who
haven't committed their thoughts to paper. If only it could be
correlated. Jean and I carefully keep records of all our patients
and, unless the cause of death is obvious, take our casualties to
the veterinary investigation centre in Aberystwyth for post
mortem. The staff there are most helpful, being willing to
explain in layman's language what has killed our erstwhile
patient as well as producing a formal report for our own vet.
Sometimes we spot something significant in a bird's behaviour
which we can relate to its survival or to the manner of its death,
and bear it in mind for the future. But we often worry that
whereas our findings are neither extensive nor scientific
enough to justify writing a paper about them, they might still be
valuable to other people. How splendid it would be if there
existed a sort of clearing house of information where this
information could be evaluated and passed on if found worthy.
The Hawk Trust manages it, so it must be possible for other
species. There was once an Association of Wild Bird Hospitals
which was going to do just what we want, but it folded for lack
of funds.

The attitude of the RSPB in this is not helpful. Unless very large numbers of birds are affected, its policy is the painless destruction of oiled seabirds. I dislike the policy, obviously, because apart from causing birds to be killed which otherwise might be saved, it is bound to make potential researchers feel 'what's the use'. Worse, it also makes the coastguard, the Naval personnel and the county Emergency Planning people, who together organize the clearing of oil spillages, feel the same way. I always pushed the birds' interests as hard as I could in any meetings I attended in my official capacity in the matter of oil pollution, but I consistently got the RSPB policy quoted to me: 'If the RSPB doesn't care, we can't.'

Birds tend to sit, impassive and expressionless and giving the hospital operator terrible trouble in diagnosis. Also, the members of any one species are very consistent – watch one guillemot and you've watched them all, with a few exceptions. Seals are different. They have some behavioural characteristics which are universal – in particular they can, better than most animals, demonstrate with total clarity when they are feeling contented. Outside those common features, though, the uniformity vanishes and every seal shows its individuality.

Seals normally move rather clumsily on land, by dragging themselves along by their front flippers, much as a prone man drags himself by his elbows. Ripple, though, used to hump along on one shoulder, not using her flippers at all, and we looked carefully for signs of injury to her flippers. Then we found her humping on the other shoulder, so we looked for evidence of a sore gut which would hurt if she lay flat. She'd had a septic umbilicus when we first had her, something which kills many seal pups, but we'd treated it and thought it had healed. Now we weren't sure. Then, one day when she was in a hurry, we found her humping along like all the others, right way up. Evidently, humping on one shoulder is only unusual, not disastrous.

Seals are very vocal, and their cries are very mournful. They usually drop from one note to another following approximately what is known in music as a minor third. Some coastal legends ascribe the cries to virgins rejoicing, but most, in view of the sadness of the minor key, associate the clamour with souls in purgatory and unhappy situations of that kind. A seal's behaviour belies the sadness of its song, but the constant association in legend of seals with human souls, in whatever condition of pleasure or pain, is probably the only reason seals have survived so long.

Vocalizing starts early in a seal's life, just as it does in a human's, and most seal pups kick up a tremendous racket right from birth. It's easy to tell the bellow of a healthy youngster which just wants its breakfast from the unhappy cry of a sick one. The cry won't tell a foster-parent what ails the sick one, but the bellow will reassure him no end. And yet, we've had four seals which never made a sound, from arrival to release in the wild.

Our records don't cover the point so I can't prove it, but my memory tells me that our noisiest babies were those which became biggest and strongest, or, more correctly, most quickly became big and strong. Moses kept up a tremendous concert for the whole five months he was with us. By now he'll be six years old, fully mature, and competing for beachmaster status, that is access to cow seals for mating. He'll have to fight an established beachmaster and displace him. Somehow, I think that if he could survive the condition he was in when we first saw him, he can do anything. He has always stood out in our minds over all the other seals we've treated, for his intelligence and his other unusual traits, not just because he was our first seal.

I've written of his antics in chapter one, but they were endless. He used to sit up with his back against something, much as you or I would sit up in bed, bent at right angles in the middle, with his flippers crossed on his chest. Quite often, when he sat up in this way, his penis, which is normally housed internally in a seal and completely out of sight, would emerge rather like a dog's and erect itself. A seal doesn't become sexually mature until it is at least five years old, so this was a most remarkable showing. No other seal has done it, and hardly any has sat up in the same way.

We got our new seal building operational in December 1979, and this has widened our horizons no end. The pool is only sixteen feet long by six wide and four deep, so a seal looks a bit like a goldfish in a bowl against the hygienic pale-blue paint, but this is infinitely better than the situation which prevailed before. A baby seal is only about three feet long, and though its girth will vary enormously it will only grow an inch or two longer in its first year, so while it is in our care it will be able to swim more or less fully in the pool. Adult seals have a habit of 'bottling', that is sleeping in a vertical position in the water. They sink to the bottom, still vertical, and every five minutes or so they rise to the surface, breathe, then sink again, sleeping all the time. We've been surprised to find a three-month baby doing this, and although it only had a foot to rise, it was definitely bottling.

When a seal has got used to us and is no longer frightened, it's possible to see exactly how it uses its flippers for swimming. It moves in the water in exactly the same way as a skin diver. It uses its hands (front flippers) for slow or careful or short movements, but its tail ones for going places. If I walk slowly along the pool, the seal inches along sideways, remaining vertical in the water, and treads water if I stand still, waiting for me to drop a fish. If I drop a fish immediately behind the seal, it spins round with a flick of a front flipper, which will be held horizontal, ready. But if I throw my fish to the far end of the pool, the seal flicks itself into the right direction with a front flipper then presses both front ones to its sides and goes after its fish using only the tail ones. A young seal can easily get going fast enough in ten feet or so to shoot right out of the water over a freeboard of six inches or so. Very occasionally, a seal pup will chase its own tail in the water and its body is so streamlined that there is only minimal disturbance at the water surface. Best of all is to watch a seal when it thinks no one is about. I honestly think that seals swim for the sheer pleasure of it. None of our seals has any real need to swim, except for a moment or two when there are fish going, and they could lie on the side all day, much warmer, and really idle. But they don't. They swim for hours on end, doing slow rolls, the odd loop, with a languorous ease which makes a mere human green with envy.

We often leave a beach ball in the pool for the seals to play with. We have two, one blue, the other yellow. Now seals are generally considered to be colour blind, but whereas a seal will sometimes push the blue ball about with its nose and flippers, no seal will go near the yellow one. There is no difference between the balls except the colour.

Seals' front flippers have five claws, in line, which they can turn into and use against a palm, so that a seal can use its flippers like a human hand with no thumb, and this makes them very dextrous. Moses could handle the little rake I made for him, with complete facility and place the end of the handle accurately in the hand of anyone he thought would scratch him with it. Seals also scratch themselves a lot, something for which their flippers are perfectly suited.

Seals have a most eloquent gesture, known as flippering, to repel someone (or another seal) for whom they have no fear, but who they think is going to do something they don't want. During the first couple of weeks of mutual acquaintance, a young seal will greet me with bared teeth and a clear intention, given half a chance, of biting my hand off. After that, though, it will accept me as a friend, a bringer of food, unless I want to get hold of it to examine it or give it an injection. A seal seems to be able to sense this kind of intention as soon as I go into the room, and it beats its flippers together, hits its chest with them and, when I get close, beats my hands furiously, too. Only when this fails to stop me does it attempt to bite me, but by that time I have usually got a decent hold on it. In the wild, a cow seal will flipper like mad at an amorous bull seal if she is not ready to mate with him and, amazingly, the gesture will be respected and the bull will go away. Amazingly, because it *is* only a gesture. There is no harm in a seal's flippers. The meaning is so clear – don't do it, don't hurt me – that I hate having to over-ride it, and I won't unless I really have to. But if a seal doesn't flipper me when I go to inject it, the treatment is probably too late.

When they are feeding themselves and all their medical troubles are over, baby seals go through a performance Jean and I call the 'goodnight ritual'. Being replete, and recognizing that feeding or whatever attention is over for the night, the baby will hump to its sleeping place. It will stretch prodigiously, roll about, raise its head and its rear end together, like an old-fashioned baby's bottle, open and close its tail flippers a few times and study them with intense interest. Note I said rear end, not tail. A seal's tail is a little stumpy thing which normally lies between the tail flippers and seems to be about as useful as a uvula in a human. It has one function, very useful when one is attending to the seal, force-feeding it, say. When it stands up straight, the seal is about to defecate.

When the seal is entirely satisfied that its rear is in good order (and its actions while it is checking explain all the legends about mermaids), it will have a good scratch. This is a leisurely operation, sometimes gentle, sometimes hard, and the baby will roll over a few times to make sure it hasn't missed anything. Then it will preen its whiskers – vibrissae, I should properly call them – one by one, until it is fully happy with those, too. Then, with its claws extended, it will run its 'hand' from the back of its neck, over its head, down its nose, and finish with its 'hand' held in front of its mouth where it may gently nibble a claw or two. It will do this several times, rolling over from time to time to maintain balance. The whole ritual takes anything from a quarter to half an hour and Jean and I love watching it. The performance is so redolent of comfort and contentment that there just can't be anything wrong with a seal that does it, and every seal of ours which has acted in this way is back in the sea in no time, fit and healthy.

There are hundreds of questions to which we want answers, about bird and animal behaviour in the wild and in temporary captivity, about methods of treatment and the diagnosis of ailments, and no doubt lots of answers will come up in time. But there is one question to which we can't imagine an answer, and if there is one it may lie in metaphysics, not biology. Birds are genetically programmed to fly, animals to run or walk, but in almost every species the parents play a vital part in teaching their offspring how to feed and how to behave in the world. Parent seals don't. They desert their pups at less than three weeks of age, without having given them any education at all. Generally nature compensates in some way for its apparent lapses but not, it seems, in this one. So why, if a seal can be genetically programmed to swim, to bottle, to flipper, to go through the 'goodnight ritual' and much more, can't there be a gene or two to teach it to eat fish?

11
Dolphins

On Wednesday, 24th March 1976, Jean and I were having a swift cup of tea at about 5.45 pm. I had just got home from work, it was a miserable day, very cold, with a slight drizzle, and beyond watching the weather forecast I had no plans for the evening. The phone rang and Jean answered it. She was back in a flash.

'Boots on,' she said. 'There's a dolphin stranded on Cei Bach.'

Cei Bach is a mile and a half away and we were there in no time. The dolphin was about a hundred yards from the ramp leading to the beach, ten yards from the edge of the tide which was falling. There were four girls with the dolphin carefully and meticulously keeping her wet using a plastic container they'd found on the high tide mark. To fill it, one them had to wade into the freezing sea. Apparently they had found her on the beach at 4.30 pm, and had carried her into three feet or so of water on the assumption that she had been stranded accidentally. Instead of swimming away, she had thrashed her way back and beached herself again. They had tried it once more but she did the same, so they decided that she was ill and needed attention. The girls were nurses, two from Radcliffe Infirmary, the other two from the Churchill Hospital, both in Oxford, staying nearby for a week's holiday.

Just at the top of the beach access ramp is a farm, Llwynon, and one of the girls had gone to it to call the RSPCA. She got hold of someone, who said he was very busy but would do what he could. He gave the impression that that wouldn't be very much, and she had gone back to the dolphin. There are no occupied properties in view of that part of the beach and it was not the sort of day to find anyone out for a casual stroll but there was one property nearby, on the cliff top, owned by a friend of ours, Jessie Ward, and it was her husband, Alan, who saw what was happening and called us.

Jean and I examined the dolphin for signs of any injury, but there were none. I opened her mouth, to see if there was any obstruction in her throat, and that was the moment when it became crystal clear that we were dealing with something entirely new, a creature totally different from any we had handled before. As I opened her mouth she cried out, not very loudly but perfectly clearly. I didn't know, of course, whether she was saying 'Don't do that. It hurts', or 'Go on, there's a hook stuck in my throat', but I did know that I was dealing with an intelligent creature, and that nothing but the best would do by way of treatment. There must be no mistakes with this one. What we didn't know we must find out, and find out correctly. I felt I was dealing with a sick person, rather than a sick animal.

The first move was to get some professional help, so I called Tom Herbert. He was out but his wife assured me that he would be along as soon as she could contact him. Although I knew I could rely on him to be as quick as he could I was biting my nails in anticipation of his arrival.

In the meantime we had to consider where to take our dolphin to look after her. A dolphin is used to being in water, having a uniform pressure all around, almost weightless. In air, all the pressure is on one side and all the organs are distorted in consequence. She had to be in water but not in too much water if she couldn't swim or even float.

She would have to lie on the bottom of whatever tank we put her in, with the greatest depth of water we could manage without covering her blow-hole. The necessity to control water depth cut out the caravan site swimming pools and the lobster tanks – in fact all the big tanks we could think of. On the other hand, as she was a common dolphin, one with a big snout, not the snub-nosed bottlenose of the dolphinariums, she was about seven feet long. Our outside tank was eight feet long, and we could adjust the water level as we liked in it. The advantages of having her at home were enormous – instant telephone, warmth, food and drink – and fortunately the outside tank was empty at the time.

I rang Hugh, and asked him to come down with the tractor and the buck rake with some seven-foot planks of timber on it – luckily we had some – and to bring a big piece of nylon trawl net which was lying about the yard. He arrived at the same time as Tom and Jackie Herbert, two families of friends who had heard what was going on, and two policemen, including the New Quay bobby, PC Jones. It transpired that the RSPCA man's response to the nurses' request for help had been to phone PC Jones and ask him what was happening. It couldn't be a dolphin, he had said, it was probably a seal, and would Jones do what he could for it? We were glad to have them all. Our only contribution to the proceedings for three quarters of an hour had been to fill the can and spray the dolphin, since Jean and I wear wearing wellingtons, and it saved the girls getting any wetter. They had refused all offers of transport to change clothes and warm up. They weren't going to abandon their dolphin for a minute.

Tom Herbert was as anxious as we were to do the right thing by our new patient. He had rung the vet of the London Zoo, who was out, and had chased him by telephone through two parties and a concert. He'd been on to Billy Smart at the Windsor Safari Park, and to the Clacton Dolphinarium. The

Clacton people were really interested and helpful, and had talked a lot of sense. On their advice, he injected as much penicillin as he would give a cow, in case of infection, and a massive dose of Vitamin B12 to allay shock. Through all this the dolphin solemnly watched us, its big eyes hardly moving.

Picking up the dolphin and carrying her was no problem, because by this time there were fourteen of us and she didn't weigh much over 200 lbs. We had to carry her a hundred yards because we couldn't get the tractor past a couple of groynes, so we put her on the net, which would curl round her and support her more evenly than a board or something hard underneath. We set her down on a thick mattress of sea weed on the platform Hugh had built on the buck rake and off we all went. I followed the tractor, whose lights had regrettably failed, with three of the nurses in their car while the other one remained on the buck rake pouring water over the dolphin.

It had not seemed at all strange to hear the four nurses and, particularly Jackie Herbert, talking to the dolphin while we were carrying it. On the contrary, it seemed perfectly natural. Just as we had her snug on the tractor, PC Jones, with a wink to me, said to the girls 'Better get the chips ready'. They were not, however, amused.

We had been amazed at the docility of our dolphin. She was immensely strong and could have made it completely impossible for us to carry her, but so far from showing her strength she had remained quiet and almost completely immobile. Apart from an occasional movement of her tail she hadn't moved on the tractor, either. Carrying her into the pool was tricky, even though we had plenty of help, because access to it had never been designed for anything seven feet long and we had to bend her a little bit to get her in. Still she didn't protest. We put her down, with her head raised a few inches on a bag of seaweed, and topped up the tank to a couple of inches below her blow hole. She started a very slight and slow rhythmic movement of her tail so we lined that end of the pool with more bags of seaweed to prevent her abrading her tail on the concrete.

We had been terribly upset to find that while carrying her in the net we had damaged her pectoral fins (called, we duly discovered, by those used to dolphins, 'pecs'). The damage was minor but it was bleeding and of course we couldn't stop it. Fortunately, it stopped on its own quite soon after we had her in cold water, to our great relief. It showed how little we knew what we were doing. Proper canvas stretchers are made to carry dolphins, with holes for the eyes, the vent, and most important, the pecs. We should have cut a couple of holes in our net.

A dolphin is a warm-blooded animal so it must keep its blood temperature constant. It cannot sweat to do this, of course, so it has a most ingenious way of adjusting its blood circulation to its level of activity to achieve the same result. When it is doing nothing in particular its blood circulates inside the insulating blubber, but when it is going at thirty knots or so, or otherwise working hard, the blood circulates through a multitude of tiny veins right up to the skin surface of the tail flippers and the fins, which have no blubber, and is cooled by the water. A dolphin out of water will heat up very quickly and soon die of heat stroke, hence the absolute necessity of a constant feed of water. It is necessary to keep all its skin wet, or it will dry out and crack, but keeping the fins and tail cool and wet is vital for a beached dolphin. A dolphin whose dorsal fin feels warm to the hand is in trouble, with a raised blood temperature. Whether this is due to lack of water cooling or whether the dolphin 'has a temperature', due to infection, is another problem, but the required action is the same – keep the fins and tail wet.

Our dolphin had been out of the sea for something like four hours before we got her into the tank and in spite of the most liberal spraying of water her fins were disturbingly warm. Her blood would therefore have been circulating in the fins and tail, in an automatic effort to cool off, hence the considerable bleeding from those very small abrasions, but once she was back in water her blood cooled down and the bleeding stopped.

Now that we had our dolphin as comfortable as we could make her, we could turn to our human problems. The girls had stayed with her all along and whereas she had been out of water four hours they had been wet to the waist for the same time. We had the makings of four cases of exposure on our hands and the girls were shivering uncontrollably when we got them indoors. Worst off was Lynn Mayor who came from Bermuda and hadn't been in this country long. Her hands were so puffy and swollen that her fingers looked like sausages. The girls were all staying in a chalet, where the only heating was one single-bar electric fire, and yet they had done all they had done in the anticipation of going back to that single-bar fire to warm up. They didn't tell us this until the next day. Penfoel was warm and the fire was bright, and together with gallons of tea and a lot of good Scotch they soon stopped shivering and went off to bath. Jean went up to find dry clothes for them and howls of laughter were soon drifting through the ceiling. When they came down I could see why. The girls were wearing either my clothes, which were mostly too long, or Jean's which were mostly too short. My sweaters looked like frocks, the inadequacies of Jean's trousers were made good with sea boot stockings, while scarves and mufflers – long-forgotten Christmas presents – covered gaps or contained oversize knitwear to the flesh beneath. I had the feeling of seeing a whole lot of girls modelling clothes at a jumble sale. Thus we sat down to a monumental mixed grill which Hugh and Diana had been cooking while the girls warmed up.

During this time, other friends had been sitting with the dolphin, for the poor thing cried pitifully if she was left alone. She gave little squeaks and clicking sounds anyway, but if we actually left her she seemed to be very distressed. Later in the night, Jean got her feet wet while she was sitting with the dolphin, but so appealing were the dolphin's cries that she sat with her wellington boots full of water for half an hour, within thirty feet of dry ones.

Soon after we got the dolphin home, Clacton rang to find out how things were going, to say it should have had enough penicillin for two cows not one, to enquire whether they could land on the little airfield attached to the RAE at Aberporth or whether they would have to fly on to Brawdy, the big naval air base near St Davids. There are no runway lights at Aberporth and the air traffic controller goes home at about 5.30 pm unless warned that something is up, so it meant Brawdy. After a searching inquisition into what we were doing the caller, Reg Bloom, who operates the dolphinarium, said he would ring again in the morning and come down then. As far as he could tell, he said, there was nothing more to be done for the time being. He also said that he and his crew had attended dolphin strandings for years. In answer to the obvious question, he said that the only one he had been able to save was a killer whale which was all wrapped up in rope and fishing net. They had just cut it free and it had swum away. I didn't pass that on to the others.

Tom Herbert and Jackie came back to deliver additional penicillin. The Windsor Safari Park rang to see how things were going. The coastguard also rang, having been told of events by the police, to say that whales, dolphins and porpoises were Queen's Fish, any stranded ones were to be reported to them, and they then informed the British Museum, Natural History section. One by one everyone left, even the nurses went at about midnight, and Jean and I were left in peace with our new friend.

We knew very little about dolphins. They can often be seen in the bay, but our knowledge of them was the result only of very general reading. I recalled one occasion when I'd got quite close to them. I had been sailing with a friend, Peter Gough, from Cardiff, in his dinghy. It was a perfect day, the sun shining and a good breeze, and we were really spanking along when we saw, ahead of us, a school of dolphins.

'In?' said Peter, at the helm, 'Or away?'

'In,' said I. 'They won't hurt us.'

So for twenty glorious minutes we sailed in the middle of a school of dolphins. If they are quite impressive playing round the bows of a liner, they present an even more imposing sight from a ten-foot dinghy with about two inches of freeboard on the lee side. They were going much faster than we were and their great backs came right out of the water within an inch or two of our gunwale. I put my hand over the side and each one rubbed its back on it. The impression given was of happy, friendly, creatures, playing with other happy creatures, whom they obviously trusted.

This memory served to enhance my determination to help this great, gentle creature for which we had assumed responsibility. I know that dolphins sometimes strand themselves because of a parasite which attacks the inner ear and destroys the dolphin's balance and orientation. Was this the trouble with this one, we wondered, and, if so, could the condition be treated? And who knew the treatment? We comforted ourselves with the thought that Clacton would be along in the morning. This was no happy, playful dolphin, but it seemed to be trusting us. It had shown no sign of aggression or even resistance when we had been handling it, unlike a seal, for instance, which would be aggressive or at least on the defensive all the time.

'Remember it's an intelligent animal,' Reg Bloom had said. 'Don't leave it alone, keep talking to it, encouraging it.'

So we talked to it, and we stroked it, softly, gently and sincerely, because we desperately wanted to save the dolphin. Stroking a dolphin is like stroking a wet wellington boot, but we never stopped – that is, until just before two in the morning, when the tail stopped moving and the breathing ceased.

Reg Bloom was on the phone before eight, and the nurses were up by a quarter past. They were inconsolable. At ten we had a call from the Natural History Museum, from the Keeper of Marine Mammals, Dr Purves. He wanted the body for research, he said, and pointed out, unnecessarily and officiously, that under the laws and regulations governing Queen's Fish he had a right to it. Could we find digs for himself and two colleagues for that night? They said they would come and fetch it.

At eleven there came a call from Cambridge University, which works closely with Clacton in dolphin research. They had heard all about our efforts from Clacton. After due com-

miseration the voice asked what was happening to the body. I
told him.

'Oh, no,' he said. 'How are they coming down?'

'In a van,' I said.

'Right,' said the voice, 'we'll beat the buggers to it. I've got
a friend with an E type.'

I said no. I didn't want World War Three starting in my
garden, not over the remains of our poor dolphin.

Dr Purves and his colleagues duly arrived and in the course
of examining the carcase he said 'young female'. I asked him
how one knew a female dolphin. There was a very long silence,
at the end of which he told me that whereas a male dolphin has
just one vent, a female has a slit each side of her vent in which
her teats are concealed. That was the only question he did
answer, in two hours or more, during which the dolphin was
moved, arranged and photographed with meticulous care from
all angles. Jean and I were bitterly disappointed. Dr Purves is a
very great authority on dolphins and whales and we had
hoped for a great deal of information from him. We got none.

On Good Friday, three weeks later, a porpoise beached
itself at Aberaeron and some students from London University,
down on holiday, found it. They told the police who told Tom
Herbert who told us, but the poor thing was dead when we got
there. A porpoise is very much smaller than a dolphin. It's only
four or five feet long, and one person can carry one easily. This
porpoise had a huge excrescence looking like a cream-coloured
sponge, four or five inches across, growing on its flank, and
parasites, looking like tiny lobsters a quarter of an inch long,
were crawling out of it, like rats leaving a sinking ship. It was a
sickening sight, and one felt that death had probably been a
blessed release to the poor creature. The vet lab found sepsis in
every part of it. The parasites created a good deal of interest,
being usually found on deep-water creatures, and never previously recorded on porpoises. This was a female, pregnant,
and not far from her time. It was easy to think of her trying
desperately to keep going long enough to drop her calf and give
it a start.

Another porpoise was brought up to us in September but it was already dead when it arrived. The post mortem showed its lungs and its stomach to be full of parasitic worms, and there were 'very many' flukes in the bile ducts, as well as areas of fibrosis in the liver.

In the same month, on Saturday 25th, to be exact, we had a phone call at about ten in the morning to say another dolphin was stranded near the life boat station in New Quay. Gareth Jones, chief engineer of the electricity board for this area, had spotted it from his boat and came ashore to call us, and when we got down there Merfyn Thomas, the mechanic of the life boat, was looking after it. It was a common dolphin, *Delphinus delphis*, like the previous one, but an inch or two longer and very much bigger and fatter.

It had already exercised its spell over people near it. A dozen or so youngsters were running furiously between it and the sea, pouring water over it from little buckets. Three or four adults were kneeling by it, all talking to it nicely, and wondering if they could stroke it. It was lying a little on its side, its breathing was very fast and its dorsal fin very hot, but it had no sign of any injury. Using the one bit of esoteric knowledge I had wrung from Dr Purves, I pronounced it to be a male – a flash of knowledge which greatly impressed the spectators, but which I instantly regretted, because everyone at once wanted to know how old the dolphin was, what it weighed, did it mate for life, where did it normally live, was its wife waiting for it and, of course, the million dollar question, why was it stranded on the beach. I looked a bit of an idiot because I had the answer to none of these questions.

Hoping desperately that the dolphin was only accidentally stranded, Hugh and I, with another local, Barry Truckell and some visitors, carried it into four feet of water. This cost me a box of matches and half an ounce of tobacco. Barry thought he was in clover. He had been working with the fishermen and so was wearing thigh boots, but waders only give you two-feet-seven of free board and he filled his boots to the top. The visitors were laughing – they were dressed for it. Just like the first one, this dolphin thrashed its way, rather awkwardly and still on its side, back up to the beach.

This time, we weren't going to risk carrying him in a net, so we put him on quite a decent door which had floated in, padded him up with seaweed and other drift wood, and borrowed a boat trailer to move him. As we moved off his spell exercised itself again. A young, attractive lady threw her arms around him and kissed him. With tears running down her cheeks she begged us to do our best for him, something we solemnly engaged to do. I was under the spell as well, but I wished she'd kissed me instead.

We took our dolphin home in the back of Hugh's pick-up, with Barry sloshing water over him all the way. Tom Herbert was waiting for us, and administered the customary penicillin and the B12. Then we carried him into the pool.

This was quite a job, because he was very much heavier than the first one, and he insisted on being just a little on one side. When we turned him up straight, inadvertently, he gave a little flick of his tail and scattered most of his carriers like skittles. It really was only a flick, but it was an indication of the power of his tail. The four of us supporting his front end nearly sank through the concrete floor before the others got a grip again. In doing this, he just touched the back of the pick-up and tore his skin. The tear was about two inches long, and showed the skin to be the better part of an eighth of an inch thick. It exposed the blubber, but there was very little bleeding because there are very few blood vessels in the blubber. Tom put some stuff on it, which, surprisingly didn't come off in the water, and in twenty-four hours the damage was nearly healed. It was an excellent demonstration both of the delicacy of a dolphin's skin, however tough and rubbery it looks, and of its recuperative powers.

We were very glad when our patient was safely in the pool. His breathing was much too fast, nearly seventy to the minute, while it should be three, and his fins were hot. Also, we had noticed a clear green liquid coming from his vent. We didn't know what that meant, but it didn't look good. We rang

Clacton, and Reg Bloom said some of his people would bring the dolphin back with them, to treat it in their sick bay pool.

This demonstration of unequivocal support warmed our hearts. There would be nothing in it for the dolphinarium except the satisfaction of helping a sick dolphin. Performing dolphins are the bottlenose variety, *tursiops truncatus*, so ours, a common dolphin, not susceptible to training, would be no value to them if they saved it.

We decided to call our dolphin Garfyn, the name being part of Gareth, who spotted him, and Merfyn, who had looked after him subsequently. We had lunch in turns, so that there was always someone with Garfyn, and Barry went home for dry clothes. At two o'clock, Reg Bloom rang to say that the van designed to carry dolphins was hopelessly broken down, that they were gutting the family dormobile to make room in it for a dolphin in a stretcher, and they would therefore be later that they had hoped. Barry came back, drier and warmer. Geoff and Yvonne Browne and their teenage children, neighbours of Tom Herbert, came over and announced that they were going to sit it out with us. Geoff runs an aquarium on the harbourside in Aberaeron.

The morning had been really lovely, but clouds had gathered and in the early afternoon the heavens opened and a fierce storm started. Hugh and I rigged corrugated sheets over the pen for a temporary roof and put concrete blocks on them to stop them blowing off. The temperature dropped fifteen degrees in half an hour, and we put on waterproof over-trousers and more sweaters. I hoped desperately for peace on the professional front. Building roads and bridges carries a high level of job satisfaction but the price of that satisfaction was being on call for twenty-four hours of every day, unless I made ad hoc arrangements with someone to stand in. If there had been flooding I would have had to turn out, dolphin or no dolphin, and the first of the autumnal storms is always the worst time for trouble. Fortunately I got the peace I had hoped for and the storm died out in the evening. By this time we had the garage inspection lamp rigged in the pen, we had planks and a few cushions to sit on, and had arrived at a reasonable working arrangement so that some of us, anyway, could be in the house in comfort.

Garfyn, all this time, had been almost motionless in his tank. His fins were still very hot, and he was still breathing far too quickly. A dolphin empties and fills its lungs in an instant, in normal circumstances in the moment that his blowhole is out of the water as he 'porpoises' along. The result is a considerable snort, and this was occurring every second. That was better than seventy, but not much. His big eye regarded us solemnly as we sprayed the bits of him that were out of the water, and talked to him. He in turn gave little squeaks and clicking noises from time to time, and he would almost certainly have been making ultrasonic noises as well. We very much regret that we never recorded him, for by re-recording reel to reel – cassette – reel to reel twice, using the two speeds on the reel-to-reel recorder, we could have dropped the pitch two octaves, which would have made his ultrasonic noises audible to humans.

At 10 pm the Brownes went home to unload the younger generation and return themselves, at 11 pm Barry went home, promising to be back at 5 am. The Clacton dormobile was somewhere around Bristol and reckoned to be with us by 2 am. So we settled down for the night, with lots of coffee and a bottle of rum.

The Clacton dormobile arrived on time bearing Anthony Bloom, the proprietor's son, and John Wilcox, diver and dolphin trainer. They came to see Garfyn straight away, and explained that the great worry was dehydration, whatever else might be the trouble. Dolphins didn't drink, they said. They got their fluids from the fish they ate, and it was a long time since this one had eaten a fish. They wondered whether to force-feed him with the mackerel we had ready-thawed or to slip a tube into his stomach and give him liquid that way. The green liquid from his vent worried them, and they settled for squirting some dianimol, much diluted, down his throat to allay the enteritis which was causing it. They said it would be best to take him back with them, because of the better facilities at Clacton.

We then ate a lot of bacon and eggs, and persuaded John to go to bed since he was doing the driving. Anthony wouldn't rest. He came out to the pool and caressed the dolphin for the rest of the night. At about half-past three we noticed a change in its behaviour. Its breathing was slower and its dorsal fin was cool. This could have been the result of the steady efforts we had all been making ever since we had it, it could have happened anyway, but – and this I am assured is very likely – it could very well have resulted from the presence of someone who knew about dolphins and was more confident with a sick one than we had been.

At 5 am Barry came back as promised, and was very welcome. At 7 am the Brownes went home, and with them went our heartfelt thanks. At 8 am, our labrador, Sheba, went upstairs and, finding John's door not fast, jumped on his bed and woke him. Fortunately it was the time he wanted to wake anyway, he said, and his own dog did the same thing to him most days at home.

Over breakfast we heard some fascinating things about dolphins from John and Anthony. They thought it quite probable that the stranding of two similar dolphins within a mile of each other and quite close in time, resulted from the first one having told his friends that a friendly and helpful reception awaited dolphins in and near New Quay. They quoted other cases of appalling things done to beached dolphins – of a man who drove his walking stick right through a live dolphin, for instance. They said it was quite well established that dolphins could communicate intelligently over very long distances, either by incredibly receptive hearing of each other's ultrasonic noises or actually by extra-sensory perception. We tried to imagine the first dolphin broadcasting that he was with a group of mad people who didn't know what on earth they were doing but were trying their best.

We helped get Garfyn ready for his long journey. He travelled in a purpose-made stretcher, like the one used to transport Nanu, the killer whale, from this country to the

States, an operation which received a lot of television coverage. It was made of very strong canvas with holes for the dolphin's eyes, pectoral fins and its vent, and was beautifully padded inside. It hung on two steel poles so that the dolphin's body was supported on each side as well as underneath. John and Anthony covered the exposed parts of him with vaseline, and we got him in the dormobile, where the stretcher hung inside a canvas bag with water in it.

Meurig Jenkins turned up at 9.30 am to record a piece for Good Morning Wales on Radio 4, and had a word with John and with me in the cab of the dormobile. John was great – he said he was planning to get Garfyn fit, bring him back and release him when there were other dolphins about. I can hear what I said, any time I care to play the tape, but I sound like a sleepwalker, two seconds between each word. You can hear Garfyn breathing away in the background.

But at least he was breathing six times to the minute at ten that Sunday morning when he left here, and our hopes were high. Whatever else, he was very much better than he had been when we first saw him. I have always found long-distance communication between dolphins difficult to accept but it is a fact that, at five to ten that morning, New Quay bay was alive with dolphins, which had been there since first light, but that five minutes after Garfyn left, there wasn't a dolphin to be seen.

Penfoel was suddenly peaceful again. The panic was over, every one had gone, the sun was shining. I had a bath and a shave, came down all nice and clean, made a cup of coffee, took up a paper. I felt great. I never finished the coffee. I was asleep in a second.

At ten that night we had a phone call from Clacton. Garfyn had died just before they got there. We felt a terrible sense of loss – less intense probably than if he'd died here, but pretty bad just the same. We'd lost seals and birds, creatures which had been with us longer and on which we'd worked harder than with Garfyn, and we had sorrowed over them when our efforts failed. Garfyn's death was like losing a close friend.

In due course we had a post-mortem report about him. His

digestive organs were fine, but his lungs were badly infected with parasitic worms which, together with various side-effects associated with their presence, had almost destroyed his capacity to breathe. No doubt the six breaths a minute he had achieved before he left here was the best he could do. His lungs did not have the capacity for three breaths a minute, like his mates. The report went on to say that the lung condition might have been made worse by a bacterial or viral infection, but the last line reads 'the probability that the animal had been affected by pesticides cannot be ruled out.' Pesticides! In the sea! God help us all.

12
Caring for Wildlife

The very thought of pesticides, or any other man-made materials, reaching a sufficiently high concentration in the sea to affect the animals, the birds and the fish that live in it, is terrifying to anyone interested in the continued existence of wild creatures. Far too many are already killed deliberately, for all sorts of reasons, but the insidious advance of pollution could well be more deadly still in the long run. There is an estimated 2,000,000 tons of DDT in the sea now, and DDT is a stable chemical so the quantity will not diminish. A substance called saxitoxin appeared in the sea off the east coast of Britain a year or two ago and decimated the population of shags and cormorants. Now, shags and cormorants feed only on fish; they are not scavengers, so there is no question of them dying from eating putrid food or picking up poisoned material by accident. The poison was in the fish they ate. Something like 10,000 guillemots died in the Irish sea a few years ago, poisoned by PCBs released from a factory somewhere in Scotland.

It can be extremely difficult to trace the source of these

poisons. The daily intake may not of itself be enough to harm the bird, but the bird will not excrete it. The poison thus lies stored in the bird's fat where it does no harm initially, but when the bird loses condition, say after being unable to feed properly in prolonged rough weather, it begins to use up its fat reserves. In this way it will transmit to its system all the accumulated toxin in a short time and the dose can then be lethal. This of course is likely to be a long way from the place the pollution occurred, and a long time afterwards.

Botulism poisoning is killing more and more birds, too. There are several kinds of botulism toxin, type A being just about the most poisonous substance known, but the one which affects birds is type C, which does not affect humans. The symptoms are extreme muscular weakness ending in paralysis, so that the bird first cannot fly, then cannot walk or swim and ultimately can't hold its head up. In America it is called Duck's disease because many ducks die of it, due, it is thought, to drinking the last drops in dried-up ponds. Over here gulls contract it, often because they feed on rubbish tips.

The best treatment is to give the birds large doses of light kaolin, which absorbs the toxin and gives them a chance to get rid of it, but if the paralysis is well advanced the birds won't survive. The vet lab has never been able to trace the toxin in birds we have treated, so we are only able to attribute the birds' deaths to botulism because their symptoms have been identical to those shown by the odd bird in which it has actually been proved.

Gulls are scavengers so they quite likely to find poisonous edibles, especially on rubbish dumps, but last June we were brought a guillemot with exactly the same symptoms. We called her Maria, and she had crawled on her wing-tips and her bill a quarter of a mile inland before she was picked up. Her legs were completely useless. We persevered with Maria and soon she was feeding herself, her wing action was fully restored, together with quite a lot of action in her legs. But her recovery didn't last and she died after six months. A guillemot only eats live fish, so where did she get the poison?

Talking of gulls, there is another problem which seems to affect that particular species but not, in our experience, any other. Someone brought us a herring gull with every appearance of brain damage. It couldn't fly or even walk properly. It simply staggered about in circles, quite obviously without proper co-ordination. We were a bit mystified, because there was no sign of physical damage or injury and we were thinking of giving the bird an overdose when Tom Herbert dropped in. He looked it over and said 'I wonder if it's vitamin deficiency. Give it lots of yeast.'

We administered the yeast accordingly, and in a week the gull was perfectly fit and flew away. We've had at least a dozen in the same state since, and yeast worked every time. Once we had a lesser black-backed gull whose head was upside-down and turned right back over its wings and even that one recovered completely in ten days. This is probably the result of the birds feeding on the local refuse tip. Seabirds could be expected to get a goodly proportion of their food by eating fish, whose livers are particularly rich in vitamins, so they would be conditioned to a high vitamin intake which they wouldn't get on the council dump.

Man is altering his environment so fast he has trouble adapting to it himself. Certainly wild species can't keep up with him and so many species are in such a delicate balance in the matter of survival that interference can be catastrophic. A little push one way and a species is on the way to extinction, a little push the other and a population explosion happens. The auks are disappearing because of oil pollution. Thor Heyerdahl has said he found lumps of oil all over every ocean he has sailed on – but gulls, taking advantage of the amount of food we throw away, are increasing in numbers at what could be considered an alarming rate.

It can be so easy. Years ago, we bought two pairs of adult fantail doves and set them up in a dovecote. Without becoming completely tame they never flew far away and they looked most attractive. But within three months a sparrowhawk had taken them all, and we were left with three baby doves without a feather between them. Jean brought them up and, with much misgiving, released them, but the same thing happened twice more, inside five years. Obviously we didn't have a viable flock. Then a pair of doves were hurt by a cat and couldn't fly properly, so we put them in an aviary, where they could live, and breed in peace and safety. They bred, in fact, prodigiously, which showed just how high the mortality of baby doves must be, even in the semi-secure conditions of a dovecote in a garden. Anyway, the efforts of that one pair pushed the numbers over the critical level, and they went on increasing for years until we now have at least a hundred doves living here and, though they still get predated regularly, the flock remains stable.

As soon as a species starts doing well, someone is sure to find a reason to complain about it. The oystercatcher is one of the most attractive of all the waterside birds and its numbers are increasing, to my delight, because I love watching them. They are fine big birds, easy to identify, with their big red bills and red legs. They often follow the edge of the rising tide, eating up small crustaceans as they get washed in, in addition to their normal diet of cockles and mussels. Their numbers have increased considerably at Penclawdd, where there are extensive commercial cockle beds, from which quite a number of people make a living. These good people complained that the stocks of cockles and, in consequence their turnover, were being much reduced by the oystercatchers and demanded that the numbers be reduced by shooting. In due course, and in spite of all the evidence that the drop in cockle population was as likely to be the result of heavy metal pollution and various other factors as of the oystercatchers, the order was given and thousands of oystercatchers were shot.

Now while I hate to have birds or anything else shot, I would not stop a cull of birds of a prolific species if their numbers and activities at a particular spot were bringing ruin to people, provided the cull was going to work. A year or two ago we tried sowing barley in the autumn instead of the spring, which is the more usual time hereabouts. As a result, our little field was ripe three weeks before any other corn for miles, and the local jackdaws found it. Jackdaws are determined birds and perched quite happily on our scarecrows, retreating only a few yards when we waved our arms and screamed at them. They went on eating our barley which remained ripe enough for them to eat, but not ripe enough to harvest. We tried shooting them but it was soon obvious that we would have to shoot all the jackdaws within commuting distance of our field to do any good. There were something like 6000 roosting in a wood half a mile away, so we gave up.

Exactly the same considerations applied at Penclawdd. Unless the cull was extended to every oystercatcher in South Wales its effect would be that of drying one end of a sponge with the other end in water. Not that the decision to cull, and what and how much to cull, would have been much influenced by considerations of the conservation of oystercatchers or cockles. The birds' future would have depended on the number of votes the sitting member of parliament might expect to lose if there was no cull, which would be many, on the number of votes the sitting party would lose if there was a 'reasonable' cull, which would not be many, and on the estimated size of the outcry which would happen if there was a real massacre. The answer was obvious – carry out a 'reasonable' cull to keep the cockle gatherers happy and not create too much of a barney with bird-lovers countrywide. And that's what happened.

An even more cynical bit of governmental interference with nature was the cull of grey seals in the Orkney Islands, ordered by the Scottish Office for the autumn of 1978. We found this hard to take, because while we were trying to save seals oiled on the Welsh coast, they were going to shoot thousands of seals up north, as a result of pressure from fishing interests. There was ample evidence that catches of commercially valuable fish had dropped round the Scottish coast, and a good deal of evidence that the seal population had increased, but there was no evidence by how much it had increased, or just how much of the drop in commercial fish catches was due to that increase.

Counting the numbers of a big flock of highly mobile birds is a formidable task, but it can be done; they are in view to be counted. But seals are different. There is no single occasion when all the seals of a given colony will be ashore together. Breeding areas will show only the fertile cows and the 'boss' bulls. Youngsters, the elderly, the unsuccessful bulls, will be somewhere else in the wide ocean. All the seals will haul out to moult, the bulls a month or so after the cows, but there are constant comings and goings and no one can say what proportion of the colony is ashore at any given time. Estimating the number of seals in a colony requires more than just counting.

It is done by a very involved calculation, based on the number of pups born in the colony in one year, something which, it is said, can be found reasonably accurately, the anticipated life of a seal, the age at which it becomes sexually mature, and so on. Different authorities apply different factors to various parts of the calculations, which is why, in the case of the notorious killing of the harp seals in Canada every year, the authorities and the hunters claim that there are many times more seals than the conservationists' figures show. The British seal population has undoubtedly increased, due first to the invention of the wellington boot which was cheaper and more waterproof than the sealskin boot, the alternative used almost universally in earlier years by seamen; and later to the various seal protection acts. Just how big is the seal population is another matter.

Counting pups, as I said, can be done reasonably accurately, but that statement does depend on the interpretation of 'reasonably'. A few years ago, the West Wales Naturalists Trust formed a grey seals group, to which I belonged, and its first agreed project was to get a firm count of pups over the coast line covered by the trust. This would have covered the west Wales colony of seals. The islands, Skomer and Ramsey, were well covered because each had a warden with a boat and a thorough knowledge of the topography. From St Davids Head to the river Teifi there are many breeding sites, in deep caves and on beaches inaccessible from the land, and only the vaguest estimates existed as to the numbers. From the Teifi to Aberystwyth there are several 'rookeries', but no estimate at all existed of the numbers. We were going to remedy this forthwith. I was to do a count from the Teifi north to New Quay.

I was shown how to do this by Sion Rees, who was then the National Park Warden for the St Davids area, and Robin Pratt, the warden of Ramsey Island. We went off in a rigid-hulled inflatable, with a big outboard motor, to do a partial count on Ramsey. There are a few open beaches on the island where breeding takes place, but for the most part the pups are to be found at the very back of the big caves, where there is a reasonably safe dry area at high tide. The island's coast line is riddled with caves, because it gets a real bashing from the sea, there being nothing much between it and America. We had a calm day for our trip, which is essential, because it would have been hopeless to try to get a boat into the caves with even a gentle groundswell running. Given a calm day, there are two things to watch for. One is to ensure that if there is a low spot in the cave roof you do not linger too long the wrong side of it on a rising tide, the other is the presence of a mother seal on the beach when you go to examine the pups. The record sheet for several beaches bore only the comment 'cow seal on station'. Visitors, however well-meaning, do not argue with over-protective mother seals.

Some of the caves split into passages like the fingers of a hand, some have only one chamber, and one cave, which is two hundred yards long at least, goes right through a headland and has a dry spot in the middle. But if there is a dry area at the back of a branch, one or more babies will be there, and, holding them by the tail flippers, we sexed them, marked them with a dye to avoid counting them twice, and recorded the numbers. Every branch of every cave with pups in it was noted on a six inch-to-a mile Ordnance Survey sheet.

There is one cave whose entrance is big enough for a liner, and where the water for a long way in is very deep. The sun was shining into the entrance as Robin pulled the boat into the shadow, about twenty yards into the cave. The water below us was brilliantly lit by the sun, and a steady procession of seals was going in and out. Our eyes were soon attuned to the shadow, so we could really see the seals moving, each one a perfect demonstration of leisurely grace and power. Robin and Sion said they had pulled up at that spot for my benefit, and I was duly grateful, but I didn't believe them. They were as enraptured by the sight as I was.

We couldn't possibly check all the breeding sites in one trip, because some caves can't be entered at high tide, and some beaches inside others can only be reached with great difficulty, unless there is enough water to float in close. So we did the ones we could reach, then had a look at some other caves, on the mainland, just out of interest, and found pups in those too. This much surprised Robin and Sion, who didn't think seals bred on that part of the coast, and they decided they would have to extend their survey quite a bit, to avoid missing anything. The afternoon had been intensely enjoyable, but it had brought home to me just what a task I had set myself. Robin had a six-inch map showing all the known breeding sites, though we had found a few new ones, but I only had a bare six-inch map. I would have to inspect every cave and inlet in eighteen miles of coast, and having located the breeding sites, visit them at least three times to count the pups on them. In fact I never started, because there was a heavy groundswell right up the coast all through September and October of that year and it was hopeless to try to get into the caves. Stephen Evans, the Nature Conservancy Council officer for Pembrokeshire did try, between Fishguard and Cardigan, but his boat overturned, and he and his boatman were very lucky to get away with it.

The Trust's seals group broke up the following year for various reasons, and has never been reactivated, so there has never been a definitive count of seal pups on the Dyfed coast. I very much doubt if there has ever been one in the Orkneys, either, but to be able to prove that there was a population trend in the seals that called for a cull would require annual counts for, say, five years, each conducted in the same way to ensure comparability of results. No such counts took place.

The Scottish Office was advised by its own scientists, by the Sea Mammal Research Unit of the National Environmental Research Council and by the Seals Advisory Committee, a statutory body set up under the 1970 Conservation of Seals Act. Nowhere on any of these august and imposing bodies was a representative of any of the wildlife conservation bodies, whose voice was therefore not heard very loudly, if at all. The Department's own scientists' report must also be suspect, because the scientist who becomes head of his section is the one who comes up with the politically correct answers. The Minister who is hell-bent on killing half the seals in Orkney for political reasons will not think much of a scientist who reports that there is no technical reason for doing it.

The cull was duly ordered, and a shipload of people hired to do the job, though in fact it was abandoned before it started. The public outcry was obviously much greater than had been anticipated. I know three people who rang up the Scottish Office and played hell, and it had its effect. Also, many people went to the rookeries with the intention of sitting amongst the seals to make shooting impossible, though it has been argued that if they had actually done so the disturbance they would inevitably have caused would have killed as many pups as the cull. And of course, Greenpeace took a hand, turning up with their ship, the *Rainbow Warrior*, and getting in the way of the ship with the marksmen.

The whole episode was a shocking example of cynical disregard for wildlife when its welfare clashed with political expediency, and it is a matter of great satisfaction that public feeling was strong enough to stop it, that there was professional support for that feeling, and that outfits like Greenpeace exist to take effective action. Twenty years ago the matter would hardly have caused an eyebrow to rise.

I think there is a changing attitude to wildlife nowadays. Twenty years ago I saw my first badger just after Jean and I moved here from Cardiff. It flopped out of a hedge right in front of me when I was driving home, late one night, and I had to do some advanced driving to avoid hitting it. I was, naturally, delighted, and I wanted to tell everyone. I soon stopped, though, because the usual reaction was 'Did you get him?' If I had the same experience today most people would be only too delighted that I'd missed.

Similarly, I was leading a little party in North Burma once – it seems a thousand years ago, now – and we stopped for the night in one corner of a clearing about the size of two tennis courts. There was impenetrable jungle behind, a river on one side. We had only two things to worry us, mosquitoes, which we could do nothing about, and Japs, who could only approach over the clearing where we would be able to handle them. It was just getting dark when the clearing filled up with elephants, dozens of them. Some were the trained timber elephants, with sawn-off tusks, which had been set free to prevent the Japs getting hold of them, others were genuine wild ones, with full tusks. Several of them came up close to have a good look at us, sticking out their trunks for a good sniff. We had weapons to hand, of course, but it never occurred to any of us even to pick up a rifle. We stood dead still, enthralled, well aware that we were having the experience of a lifetime. Within a few minutes they had all wandered off and we were left with an empty clearing. No one said anything for some time. It had hardly seemed real. And yet, just as in the case of the badger, many people I have told this to have asked, 'Did you manage to get one of them?'

I used to despair, but I feel the climate is changing and people are now keener to shoot wildlife with cameras than they are with guns. People are thrilled to see a badger, or a peregrine, or even a seal. They bring us sick or injured birds from amazing distances or call us for advice. Our local commercial fishermen are strong supporters of the local seals because of the summer visitors they take to see them, just as, now that whaling is prohibited in Hawaii, the inhabitants find that it is more profitable to take visitors to see the whales than it used to be to kill them.

I wish it was possible to prohibit totally the killing of

whales. This seems to be one area in which conservation is not getting very far, because of course it is tied up with profits, and governments, and politics. Greenpeace is doing a marvellous job in this, by getting between a threatened whale and the hunter ship, in inflatable boats, so making it impossible to harpoon the whale. This is the epitome of passive resistance and it will undoubtedly work in the end, given support. I must say, though, that I would prefer something more militant. I used to watch, on television, our ships keeping the Icelandic gunboats away from the British trawlers during the cod war, thinking always how splendidly those tactics would frustrate a whaler. My heart warmed to the man who bought a trawler, filled her bows with concrete and rammed the pirate whaler, the *Sierra*, putting her out of action for months, and to the man who blew her up as soon as she was repaired, and sank her in Lisbon harbour. I would like to see a warship calling over the loud-hailer to a whale hunter – 'Shoot that whale and I blow your bows off.' It's a lovely thought but unlikely to be fulfilled. I doubt if even Jimmy Saville could fix that one.

It hurts badly to find the government spending quite considerable sums to have birds and seals killed when Jean and I and people like us are trying to save individual members of the very species that have been condemned, particularly where the justification for the slaughter is very shaky. It throws grave doubts on the commitment of government to the conservation of wildlife, for all that it has established the Nature Conservancy Council and other bodies to do research into the matter. Government seems to ignore the findings of its own people, if it appears to be expedient to do so. But these things also cast doubts over the effectiveness of the efforts of people like us.

Are we actually effective? The question is valid and deserves consideration. We make quite considerable efforts to save sick and injured birds, and so on, and if we were doing no good it would be better to direct our efforts to some other channel. It would be better if the funds we spend, and which are contributed by supporters all over the country as well as hereabouts, were spent differently.

Jean and I think our efforts are effective, and friends and supporters do so, too. We've saved hundreds of birds, and quite a few seals, which would certainly have died without us. It may not sound much but we derive so much pleasure from watching these creatures in their natural state that looking after some of them when they need care is a small price to pay for the privilege. Also there is no small satisfaction in watching clean birds which were once oiled swimming away, or an injured bird fly or a seal return to the sea. It is tremendously satisfying accurately to spot what ails a bird and to watch it respond to treatment.

On the basis of cost effectiveness, that goal and ambition of present-day management, we, and wildlife generally, are on shaky ground. Who is to put a value, in pounds sterling, on a buzzard, or a robin, or a dolphin? Some authorities in some places assign a negative value to wildlife – the bounty for dead oystercatchers at Penclawdd was 25p. Over the counter a wild creature, and I mean a wild creature *in* the wild, not a captive or a tame one, has no monetary value, so all too many people accord it no importance. I know some who would kill every bird that flies if so doing would bring them a fiver. Fortunately and praise the Lord for it, more and more people do accord a high value to wildlife in its proper environment. They feel that their lives would be very much poorer with no birds, no seals, no whales, and are willing to make considerable efforts to preserve the wild creatures. We like to think we have swayed a few people that way.

Treating birds is, like all interesting activities, a matter of highlights and shadows, of success and failures, of rejoicing and sorrow. Certainly it is not the uniform grey existence to which modern town life seems to be leading. Jean and I are fortunate in that our successes loom larger in our memories than our failures. To have a bird die after weeks of treatment is depressing. By that time it has become something of a family pet, we know its likes and dislikes and try to please it. But one good walk on a favourite beach and we are ourselves again. An unexpected cash contribution, say, or the arrival of a new patient over which someone has obviously taken a great deal of trouble, and we are back in the clouds.

Tom Herbert brought in a black-headed gull one day, with no obvious ailment save that it couldn't fly, and as usual we asked him what he wanted to call it. 'Look at those lovely long slim legs,' he said. 'We'll call it Angela, after Angela Rippon.' At that time, Tom was suffering badly from 'flu, and his wife was driving him about because he had double vision. He should have been in bed but his partner was away. Now he had been a great admirer of Miss Rippon ever since the famous Morecambe and Wise Christmas show, so Jean said she would write to her and tell her she had a new namesake, and duly did. This was long before she nailed her colours to the countrylover's mast with her television programme, so we were delighted to get a charming letter from her a few days later, wishing her *alter ego* a rapid return to where she belonged. It cured Tom's 'flu.

One type we can do without, though luckily there aren't too many about, is the pompous and over zealous do-gooder. We met a beauty once. Jean and I were returning a de-oiled gannet called Screwball to the sea. We had him in an enormous carton, well tied up and had just got to our chosen secluded spot when suddenly a man turned up and in a voice of doom said 'You've got something alive in that box. I demand to see what it is.'

I shrugged my shoulders and began untying the string. I advised our friend to stand back a bit but he wouldn't so I opened the lid. Up came Screwball like a jack in the box and the chap went straight over backwards. Screwball went away merrily, diving and preening, but our new acquaintance was most put out. Now if I had accosted a stranger whom I thought was going to drown some puppies, say, and found that in fact he'd cleaned an oiled bird which he was about to release, I would have been delighted. But not this chap. He was very disgruntled. A few moments later he missed a sight that's seldom seen. When Screwball was about a hundred yards out a little school of dolphins went past and one of them, incredibly, came up right under him and flipped him a couple of feet into the air with its tail. Screwball was not in the least put out. He paddled on without turning his head.

Many people take injured birds and animals to the nearest Police Station, not knowing what else to do, and the police are always very good about it. Usually we get a phone call asking for advice, and if the advice is 'get the bird to us', we generally ask whether there is a patrol car coming our way in the reasonably near future. It isn't usually long before a police car turns up complete with 'patient'. During the later days of the *Christos Bitas* incident when oiled birds were coming in all over the coast, police headquarters in Aberystwyth asked for ponchos and immediate treatment medicine for the birds brought in there. 'Don't worry about boxes,' they said, 'We'll find boxes!' One policeman in Aberystwyth once risked his neck in very rough seas to get hold of a baby seal with a bad wound.

I think of that episode, of the dedication of the Oxford nurses to their dolphin, of all the people who patrolled the beaches to bring in the birds oiled by the *Christos Bitas*, of the people who faithfully came to our Open Day and keep us going financially, and reflect that society is not wholly without care for its wildlife. Naturally, I would like to see more people caring, but enough people do care to eliminate the lonely feeling Jean and I used to have when first we cleaned oiled birds.

As an inspiration to waverers I quote the Greenpeace watchword, which explains the name of its ship, the *Rainbow Warrior*. It is itself a quotation from ancient Red Indian lore, and it reads – 'When the Earth is sick and the animals disappear, the Warriors of the Rainbow will come to protect the wildlife and heal the Earth.'

Index

Anglesey, Lady, 61
aspergillosis, 44, 51, 103
auks (*see also* guillemots, puffins, razorbills), 65, 114
Austin, Tom, 126, 127, 128

barn owls, 80–2
Batten, Adrian, 112
Beached Bird Survey, 72
Biggles (buzzard), 85–6
bitumen, 117–18
Bloom, Anthony, 179
Bloom, Reg, 173–8
Bonnie (seal), 126
Bottle (heron), 138–9, 140
botulism poisoning, 184
Bowen, Rosemary, 90
BP1100 X emulsifier, 159
British Seals (Hewer), 153–4
Browne, Geoff, 178
Browne, Yvonne, 178
Bruce, Phyllis, 28
buzzards, 26–8, 84–6, 88–9

Calvert, Brig. J. M., 76
Cambridge University, 175
Cardigan Wildlife Park, 140
Charles, Prince, 61, 62
Christos Bitas oiling, 140–51, 158–9
Clacton Dolphinarium, 169–70
Coedmor Wildlife Park, 109
Conservation of Seals Act (1970), 191
cormorants, 72–3
Crosswell, Dave, 141
Croxall, Dr, 148, 160
Cullen, Malcolm, 15, 17

Davies, John, 19, 142
Davies, Ken, 119, 120, 141
Davies, Peter, 44, 108, 125, 138
Davies, Phil, 141
DDT in sea, 183–4
Degenhard, Kevin, 128
dehydration, 51

Delphinus delphis, see under dolphins, 176
Denim (gannet), 121, 122, 127
detergents, 36
Dickie (guillemot), 58–9
diesel fuel, 52–4, 58
dolphins: bottlenose (*Tursiops truncatus*), 178; common (*Delphinus delphis*), 71, 167–75, 176–82
doves (*see also* pigeons) fantail, 185–6
Droopy (peregrine), 90
Duncan (buzzard), 26–8
Dylan (seal), 133–4

eagles, 94
Evans, Elaine, 144
Evans, Ivor, 144
Evans, Mrs Myfanwy, 87
Evans, Stephen, 105, 133, 142, 190
Evans, Winston, 131

Falkus, Hugh, 156
fantail doves, 185–6
First Aid and Care of Wild Birds (Croxall), 160
Flake (seal), 96–7
Flawn, Helen, 145
fledglings, 24
Flipper (seal), 150–1
fulmars, 73–4

Gan (gannet), 67–70
gannets, 65, 66–70, 121–2, 125, 126, 195
Garfyn (dolphin), 176–82
Glyn (buzzard), 88–9
golden eagles, 94
Greenmount Bird Hospital, 64
Greenpeace organization, 191, 193, 196
Griffiths, 'Muffs', 89–90, 111
guillemots, 30–3, 37–48, 58–9, 130; poisoned, 184; research